999

The Wisdom of
SARTRE

A Selection

Also available from The Wisdom Library

THE WISDOM OF GANDHI
THE WISDOM OF GIBRAN
THE WISDOM OF THE KABBALAH
THE WISDOM OF THE KORAN
THE WISDOM OF MUHAMMAD
THE WISDOM OF SARTRE
THE WISDOM OF THE TALMUD
THE WISDOM OF THOREAU

Published by Citadel Press

The Wisdom of
SARTRE

A Selection

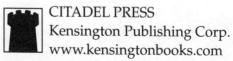

CITADEL PRESS
Kensington Publishing Corp.
www.kensingtonbooks.com

The present selection is from the main work of Jean-Paul Sartre, *L'Etre et le Néant (Being and Nothingnesss)* as translated by Hazel E. Barnes.

CITADEL PRESS books are published by Kensington Publishing Corp., 850 Third Avenue, New York, NY 10022. Citadel Press and its logo are trademarks of Kensington Publishing Corp.

Titles included in the Wisdom Library are published by arrangement with Philosophical Library.

All Kensington titles, imprints, and distributed lines are available at special quantity discounts for bulk purchases for sales promotions, premiums, fund raising, educational, or institutional use. Special book excerpts or customized printings can also be created to fit specific needs. For details, write or phone the office of the Kensington special sales manager: Kensington Publishing Corp., 850 Third Avenue, New York, NY 10022, attn: Special Sales Department, phone 1-800-221-2647.

First Wisdom Library printing May 2001

10 9 8 7 6 5 4 3 2 1

Printed in the United States of America

Cataloging data for *The Wisdom of Sartre* may be obtained from the Library of Congress.

ISBN 0-8065-2250-X

The Wisdom of
SARTRE

A Selection

THE WISDOM OF SARTRE

Wade Baskin, Professor of Modern Languages
Southeastern State College

The wisdom of Jean-Paul Sartre has found partial expression in a stream of words which now fill more than thirty volumes. Forever exploring new path-ways to freedom, his thought transcends the limitations of class or nationality and encompasses problems common to all mankind. Though he would be the first to reject the label, those familiar with his activities call him an apostle of humanistic existentialism. His indefatigable efforts to relate his doctrine to the practical demands of living are reflected in his contributions to social and political philosophy. His uniqueness resides in his ability to use these original contributions to philosophy in creating works of the highest literary merit. His incisive words strike a responsive chord in the hearts of all men committed to the defense of human freedom and unwilling to concede, with the philosopher Michel Foucault, that not merely God but man himself—the humanist's man—is dead.

"I was prepared at an early age to regard teaching as a priesthood and literature as a passion," he wrote in his remarkable autobiography, *The Words*. Books were his companions and playthings. The library was a universe captured in a mirror. He wrote his first novel at the age of eight, and he has never ceased to explore the possibilities of words. He turns with ease from creative literature to technical philosophy. His novels and plays go beyond mere illustration and elaborate concepts simply mentioned in passing or abandoned as unproductive in his formal studies. His vast output, noteworthy alike for its stylistic perfection and infinite variety, is unified by his unique vision of man in the existential situation. In his novels, dramas, essays, and philosophical treatises he studies the unique source of human misery and human grandeur—human freedom. The complexity of the Sartrean universe is the reflection of the personality of an extraordinary man with a single purpose: to play a constructive role in the universal drama in which the outcome depends on man's awareness and commitment of his freedom.

Jean-Paul Sartre was born in Paris on June 21, 1905. Orphaned shortly after his birth, the ugly, walleyed boy was brought up by his grandfather, Charles Schweitzer, an uncle of the great missionary. The books to which Sartre was exposed early in life were those venerated by his grandfather's generation and placed in the patriarch's library. Early in life Sartre was overwhelmed by the idea that salvation could be found through literary creation, but he rejected the bourgeois Catholic morality of his own generation. As a student at the École Normale Supérieure he reacted against the prevailing mood of Cartesian rationalism; moreover, he shared the surrealists' delight in overturning bourgeois values and reversing meaning by identifying reality with the world of imagination and dream. He received his doctorate in philosophy, with high honors, in 1929 and embarked upon a successful teaching career. He taught in the provincial secondary schools for several years, but he was able occasionally to travel—to Egypt, Greece, Italy, and Germany—always absorbing ideas. It was in Germany that he became interested in the work of Edmund Husserl, Martin Heidegger, and Soren Kierkegaard. After his return from his period of study in Germany, he published his first philosophical and fictional works—a treatise on the *Imagination* (1936), and an epochal novel, *Nausea* (1938). He gave up his teaching position at the Lycée Pasteur in Neuilly and enlisted as a private in the army when World War II broke out. Sent to the Maginot Line, he was captured and held prisoner for several months (1940–41). Following his repatriation, he returned to his post at the Lycée Pasteur. He moved from there to the Lycée Condorcet in Paris, where he also played an active role in the resistance movement. His first play, *The Flies* (1943), was a protest against tyranny, yet he was able to have it produced in France during the German occupation. During the same year he outwitted the censors and published his monumental treatise on phenomenological ontology, *Being and Nothingness.* Vitally interested in political movements after the liberation, he founded *Les Temps Modernes* (1946), which publishes many of his works and serves as a platform for the expression of independent left-wing views. A legendary figure even before his major philosophical work had been translated into English (his plays had drawn huge audiences, and his essays and other fictional works, including the first volume of his *Roads to Freedom,* had captured the imagination of the younger generation), he traveled widely throughout the United States and lectured at various universities. His words of wisdom made him the undisputed leader of the French intellectuals of his generation. In 1949 he helped to found the Republican Democratic Rally, which collapsed in 1952. Undaunted, he has continued to turn out essays, novels, plays, and scenarios which define and dramatize existentialist views. That he has alienated many Americans in recent years—by allying himself with the War Crimes Tribunal initiated by Lord Russell, for instance, and by condemning our foreign policy as well as our handling of such domestic issues as desegregation—is undeniable. We might recall that he was no less outspoken in his condemnation of Stalinist prison camps and Soviet intervention during the Hungarian uprising. At any rate, we should credit him with complete honesty in his attempt to achieve the goal which he set for himself in his first major exposition of the philosophy of existentialism: to use his own freedom "to modify the shape of the world."

The roots of existentialism are broad and deep. While the philosophy generally associated with Sartre's name is an epitome of a mood of our time, it is as old as man's desire to understand himself and his surroundings. There are two opposing views of human existence, the absurd and the tragic. One who adopts the absurd view concludes that human existence is ultimately futile and without meaning, a vain challenge to the void. One who adopts the tragic view discovers purpose and meaning in the struggle to understand himself and his surroundings. It is from the latter view that Sartre now observes the human drama. Through the years he had moved from the concept of "man as a useless passion" incapable of respecting the freedom of others to the view that each man, in pursuing his own freedom, must pursue the freedom of all men.

The cataclysm of two world wars produced a somber vision of human existence and made people throughout the world receptive to the dark elements of existentialist thought: alienation, self-deception, anguish (the dread of freedom or of nothingness), introspection, contingency, responsibility. It was Sartre who wedded these elements into a system and—with his novels, plays, and scenarios and critical studies—chaneled into the mainstream of artistic creation notions which had preoccupied philosophers since the days of Heraclitus.

The first popular exposition of Sartre's views are found in *Nausea*, the celebrated novel which marked a turning point in French fiction. Here existence acquires a new meaning as Antoine Roquentin, a writer, reduces it to consciousness of existence and is sickened by the chaotic, viscuous quality of his surroundings.

Overcome when he realizes that the things around him are simply there, grotesque and meaningless, Roquentin feels totally alienated, unable to classify or confer meaning on things or events. He yearns for a solid, predictable universe to rid him of his nausea. He experiences the horror of life in the absurdity of its proliferation and longs to transcend things or to reduce them to instruments for his own use. He discovers that people hide behind their status symbols, that activities and incidents are meaningless until an unpredictable future confers significance upon them, that his life cannot be a succession of discrete, orderly moments, and, finally, that the world is wholly contingent, with the result that human existence requires him to exercise his freedom to confer meaning on his own life. Through art he may find salvation. By using his imagination to create a perfect world, he may make a commitment which will give meaning to his existence and enable him to look upon his own past without disgust.

Readers quickly identified Roquentin with Sartre and confidently expected the philosopher to go beyond raising the hope of personal salvation, justification, or redemption through art. The journey from aesthetic hope to the rediscovery of man's true humanity—"the power to make history by pursuing his own ends," as Sartre puts it in his *Search for a Method* (1957)—is still incomplete. It is obvious, however, that Roquentin, the existentialist anti-hero, continues to appeal to today's youth, who are quick to show their aversion to the pretense, self-deceit, and hypocrisy which they detect at every level of existence. Their "nausea" finds expression in the renunciation of contemporary values based on the absurd competitiveness which ensnares their elders, and in their espousal of the belief that honesty is a virtue, phoniness a vice.

Nausea was an initial statement of an emergent doctrine which found systematic expression in *Being and Nothingness*, which represents both a massive attempt to construct an existentialist theory of being and an exhaustive study of man as the central object of philosophical inquiry. Even though it clearly exhibits strains of Kierkegaardian pessimism, Hegelian-Marxist dialectics, and German phenomenology, it bears the stamp of its author's unique vision. From Kierkegaard, Sartre borrowed the image of man's anguish—his awareness of his own alienation or estrangement, his abandonment in an absurd world. From Hegel came the antithetical notions of unconscious beings who exist only *in themselves* and of conscious beings who are capable of transcending the immediate situation by making meaningful choices leading to the attainment of projected goals, and who therefore exist *for themselves* and are necessarily free. Marxism inspired Sartre's passion for action, and phenomenology his compulsion to dissect consciousness, and analyze the experiences which enable the conscious being to apprehend the hostile environment into which he is haplessly flung.

Sartrean existentialism assumes that man is born into a hostile world, becomes aware of his utter loneliness, and discovers that his human freedom is the source of both his misery and his grandeur. In his vision we see a reflection of Pascal's image of man, weak in body but conscious of his awesome power as a thinking being. Man is free to act, to choose, and to project meaningful goals. The individual's choices determine his *existence,* which Sartre views as an active process, an emergence from passiveness. *Essence,* which commonly refers to something possessed by all members of a single species, refers to the result achieved by the conscious exercise of freedom. Consequently man truly exists only in so far as he consciously shapes his own existence, and the famous formula, "Existence precedes essence," acquires real meaning. Though man is flung into a hostile, meaningless universe, he is able to use the awesome power of his consciousness to fashion a habitable environment for himself. The meaning and value of the world depends on his existential choice, which may be buried in a lower level of consciousness but must be discovered before he can become truly alive. Each man lives in a world of his own or, in existentialist terms, creates his own situation. An existential subject—one who is aware of his misery and his grandeur, his forlornness and his unlimited freedom—knows that he must bear alone the responsibility for his acts.

The existential subject is overawed by his dreadful freedom, but he can mitigate his anguish by freely assuming a positive role in human affairs. The concept of salvation through commitment is elaborated most forcefully in Sartre's fictional works, particularly his plays. As a dramatist Sartre has scored his greatest popular successes, and it is for the theater that he has created his most enlightening situations. The actor in one of his plays is typically free in a given situation, faces the moment of free choice, suffers the fate dictated by his choice. Since Sartre holds that drama exists only when all spectators are bound by a common unity, he chooses situations which are familiar to all. A recurrent theme in practically every Sartrean drama is that man must commit himself wholly (he must soil his hands) if he is to make maximum use of his freedom, the only attribute which "makes man like God." For example, *The Flies* (1943) based on the Orestes legend, condemns tyranny and stresses the necessity of making choices; *No Exit* (1944), analyzes the plight of victims of self-deceit; *Dirty Hands* (1948) refutes the notion that ends justify means; and *The Devil and the Good* holds out the hope that the existential subject's estrangement can be overcome by human love. "It is enough for a man to love all other men with undivided love," says the protagonist. "This love will spread to all mankind." The implications of the existentialist view of human freedom and commitment also form the substructure of the series of novels published under the general title *Roads to Freedom* (1945———) and of many of his writings covering a wide range of subjects—literature, aesthetics, economics sociology and politics.

Each of Sartre's major works, whether technical or creative, is a call to action. The function of a writer, according to him, is to call a spade a spade, to communicate accurately and effectively with his audience. He does this even when he deals with taboo subjects, as in *Saint Genet* (1952), or incurs the wrath of all those affected by his words. Even those who disagree radically with his contentions are forced to respect the clarity of his arguments and the skill with which he wields his trenchant weapon—words. He cherishes his own freedom as a writer too much to ally himself with any organized groups. It was not without justification that he refused the 1964 Nobel prize for literature. The Academy praised his "authorship, which has always been rich in ideas and which has had a vast influence on our times, mainly through its spirit of liberty and quest for truth." Sartre's refusal was based on the conviction that "a writer must refuse to allow himself to be transformed into an institution, even if it takes place in the most honorable form." He argued with Gallic logic that "any statement attributed to Jean-Paul Sartre, Nobel prize winner," would not have the same effect as one signed merely with his name.

It is as a free man that he defends his own freedom and urges all men to pursue their search for freedom. The real impact of his most recent writings may be, not in the literate, industrialized nations, but in the third world, where the pursuit of freedom appeals to large masses. The *Critique of Dialectical Reasoning* (1961), which he regards as his major theoretical work, is widely read and understood today by intellectuals engaged in the struggle against colonialism. He identifies himself with these intellectuals and with "groups in fusion" in Africa, Asia, and Latin America. His sympathy is with spontaneously organized groups, bodies of men whose goal is a single action. These groups provide the existential subject with an opportunity to commit his freedom to the shaping of historical action. They are not yet "bureaucratized," and their very instability and insufficiency, like Giacometti's fragile, elfin sculptures, rule out any sustained engagement. Democracy, he argues, is only a façade; the real conflicts of our time, struggles based on conflicting interests of groups, are resolved outside the framework of democracy. The same principle applies to economic and social theories: they are intelligible only to those who have committed their freedom to the struggle for independence and are subordinate to the practical judgments which activists must make in dealing with a particular situation. Though denied an active role in the historical process, people in the free world should support those engaged in colonial struggle. The *Critique,* a long and at times baffling study, is presented as a needed supplement to Marxism, which subordinates the role of the individual consciousness in the historical process and stresses the external circumstance which determine man's fate. Its impact upon third-world intellectuals and activists will be the measure of Sartre's success in revitalizing Marxism.

The Words (1964) marks a return to Cartesian clarity of expression. In this autobiographical work, Sartre offers a word-portrait of his own psyche and temperament, a brilliant analysis of the evolution of the mind of a genius. He does not refuse his earlier views but now finds that experience has brought about a change of emphasis. He writes that he has "experienced reality" and "seen children dying of hunger. *Nausea* diminishes in importance at the sight of a dying child."

As Morris Bishop has observed in speaking of Voltaire and the eighteenth century, we may wonder whether Jean-Paul Sartre is actually determining the spirit of his age or is "merely the incarnation and symbol of a prevailing state of mind." Sartre's wisdom sparkles in its myriad setting. From the nihilistic view of man as a "useless passion" with no other destiny than the destiny "which he forges for himself on this earth," he has moved on the precept that a man who chooses freedom for himself rediscovers his true humanity, for by his choice he chooses freedom for all men. Words continue to flow from Sartre's pen, but even if, today, he ceased to write, he would nevertheless transcend his moment in human history.

THE WISDOM OF SARTRE

A SELECTION

THE problem of the body and its relations with consciousness is often obscured by the fact that while the body is from the start posited as a certain *thing* having its own laws and capable of being defined from outside, consciousness is then reached by the type of inner intuition which is peculiar to it. Actually if after grasping "my" consciousness in its absolute interiority and by a series of reflective acts, I then seek to unite it with a certain living object composed of a nervous system, a brain, glands, digestive, respiratory, and circulatory organs whose very matter is capable of being analyzed chemically into atoms of hydrogen, carbon, nitrogen, phosphorus, *etc.*, then I am going to encounter insurmountable difficulties. But these difficulties all stem from the fact that I try to unite my consciousness not with *my* body but with the body of *others*. In fact the body which I have just described is not *my* body such as it is *for me*. I have never seen and never shall see my brain nor my endocrine glands. But because I who am a man have seen the cadavers of men dissected, because I have read articles on physiology, I conclude that my body is constituted exactly like all those which have been shown to me on the dissection table or of which I have seen colored drawings in books. Of course the physicians who have taken care of me, the surgeons who have operated on me, have been able to have direct experience with the body which I myself do not know. I do not disagree with them, I do not claim that I lack a brain, a heart, or a stomach. But it is most important to choose the *order* of our bits of knowledge. So far as the physicians have had any experience with my body, it was with my body *in the midst of the world* and as it is for others. My body as it is *for me* does not appear to me in the midst of the world. Of course during a radioscopy I was able to see the picture of my vertebrae on a screen, but I was outside in the midst of the world. I was apprehending a wholly constituted object as a *this* among other *thises,* and it was only by a reasoning process that I referred it back to being *mine;* it was much more my *property* than my being.

It is true that I see and touch my legs and my hands. Moreover nothing prevents me from imagining an arrangement of the sense organs such that a living being could see one of his eyes while the eye which was seen was directing its glance upon the world. But it is to be noted that in this case again I am the *Other* in relation to my eye. I apprehend it as a sense organ constituted in the world in a particular way, but I can not "see the seeing;" that is, I can not apprehend it in the process of revealing an aspect of the world to me. Either it is a thing among other things, or else it is that by which things are revealed to me. But it can not be both at the same time. Similarly I see my hand touching objects, but do not *know* it in its act of touching them. This is the fundamental reason why that famous "sensation of effort" of Maine de Biran does not really exist. For my hand reveals to me the resistance of objects, their hardness or softness, but not *itself*. Thus I see my hand only in the way that I see this

inkwell. I unfold a distance between it and me, and this distance comes to integrate itself in the distances which I establish among all the objects of the world. When a doctor
takes my wounded leg and looks at it while I, half raised up
on my bed, watch him do it, there is no essential difference
between the visual perception which I have of the doctor's
body and that which I have of my own leg. Better yet, they
are distinguished only as different structures of a single
global perception; there is no essential difference between
the doctor's perception of *my* leg and my own present perception of it. Of course when I touch my leg with my finger,
I realize that my leg is touched. But this phenomenon of
double sensation is not essential: cold, a shot of morphine,
can make it disappear. This shows that we are dealing with
two essentially different orders of reality. To touch and to be
touched, to feel that one is touching and to feel that one is
touched—these are two species of phenomena which it is
useless to try to reunite by the term "double sensation." In
fact they are radically distinct, and they exist on two incommunicable levels. Moreover when I touch my leg or when I
see it, I surpass it toward my own possibilities. It is, for example, in order to pull on my trousers or to change a dress-
ing on my wound. Of course I can at the same time arrange
my leg in such a way that I can more conveniently "work"
on it. But this does not change the fact that I transcend it toward the pure possibility of "curing myself" and that consequently I am present to it without its *being me* and
without my *being it*. What I cause to exist here is the *thing*
"leg;" it is not the leg as the *possibility which I am* of walking,
running, or of playing football.

Thus to the extent that my body indicates my possibilities in the world, seeing my body or touching it is to transform these possibilities of mine into dead-possibilities. This
metamorphosis must necessarily involve a complete *this-*

ness with regard to the body as a living possibility of running, of dancing, *etc.* Of course, the discovery of my body as an object is indeed a revelation of its being. But the being which is thus revealed to me is its *being-for-others*. That this confusion may lead to absurdities can be clearly seen in connection with the famous problem of "inverted vision." We know the question posed by the physiologists: "How can we set upright the objects which are painted upside down on our retina?" We know as well the answer of the philosophers: "There is no problem. An object is upright or inverted in relation to the rest of the universe. To perceive the whole universe inverted means nothing, for it would have to be inverted in relation to something." But what particularly interests us is the origin of this false problem. It is the fact that people have wanted to link *my* consciousness of objects to the body of the Other. Here are the candle, the crystalline lens, the inverted image on the screen of the retina. But to be exact, the retina enters here into a physical system; it is a *screen* and only that; the crystalline lens is a *lens* and only a lens; both are homogeneous in their being with the candle which completes the system. Therefore we have deliberately chosen the physical point of view—*i.e.*, the point of view of the outside, of exteriority—in order to study the problem of vision; we have considered a dead eye in the midst of the visible world in order to account for the visibility of this world. Consequently, how can we be surprised later when consciousness, which is absolute interiority, refuses to allow itself to be bound to this object? The relations which I establish between the Other's body and the external object are *really* existing relations, but they have for their being the being of the for-others; they suppose a center of intra-mundane flow in which knowledge is a *magic* property of space, "action at a distance." From the start they are placed in the perspective of the Other-as-object.

If then we wish to reflect on the nature of the body, it is necessary to establish an order of our reflections which conforms to the order of being: we can not continue to confuse the ontological levels, and we must in succession examine the body first as being-for-itself and then as being-for-others. And in order to avoid such absurdities as "inverted vision," we must keep constantly in mind the idea that since these two aspects of the body are on different and incommunicable levels of being, they can not be reduced to one another. Being-for-itself must be wholly body and it must be wholly consciousness; it can not be *united* with a body. Similarly being-for-others is wholly body; there are no "psychic phenomena" there to be united with the body. There is nothing *behind* the body. But the body is wholly "psychic." We must now proceed to study these two modes of being which we find for the body.

I. THE BODY AS BEING-FOR-ITSELF FACTICITY

IT appears at first glance that the preceding observations are opposed to the givens of the Cartesian *cogito*. "The soul is easier to know than the body," said Descartes. Thereby he intended to make a radical distinction between the facts of thought, which are accessible to reflection, and the facts of the body, the knowledge of which must be guaranteed by divine Providence. It appears at first that reflection reveals to us only pure facts of consciousness. Of course on this level we encounter phenomena which appear to include within themselves some connection with the body; "physical" pain, the uncomfortable, pleasure, *etc.* But these phenomena are no less *pure facts of consciousness*. There is a tendency therefore to make *signs* out of them, affections of consciousness occasioned by the body, without realizing that one has thereby irremediably driven the body out of consciousness and that no bond will ever be able to reunite this body, which is already a body-for-others, with the consciousness which, it is claimed, makes the body manifest.

Furthermore we ought not to take this as our point of departure but rather our primary relation to the in-itself: our being-in-the-world. We know that there is not a for-itself on the one hand and a world on the other as two closed entities for which we must subsequently seek some explanation as to how they communicate. The for-itself is a relation to the world. The for-itself, by denying that it is being, makes there be a world, and by surpassing this negation toward its own possibilities it reveals the "thises" as instrumental-things.

But when we say that the for-itself is-in-the-world, that consciousness is consciousness *of* the world, we must be careful to remember that the world exists confronting consciousness as an indefinite multiplicity of reciprocal relations which consciousness surveys without perspective and contemplates without a point of view. *For me* this glass is to the left of the decanter and a little behind it; *for Pierre,* it is to the right and a little in front. It is not even conceivable that a consciousness could survey the world in such a way that the glass should be *simultaneously* given to it at the right and at the left of the decanter, in front of it and behind it. This is by no means the consequence of a strict application of the principle of identity but because this fusion of right and left, of before and behind, would result in the total disappearance of *"thises"* at the heart of a primitive indistinction. Similarly if the table leg hides the designs in the rug from my sight, this is not the result of some finitude and some imperfection in my visual organs, but it is because a rug which would not be hidden by the table, a rug which would not be either under it or above it or to one side of it, would not have any relation of any kind with the table and would no longer belong to the "world" in which *there is* the table. The in-itself which is made manifest in the form of the *this* would return to its indifferent self-identity. Even space as a purely external relation would disappear. The constitution of space as a multiplicity of reciprocal relations can be effected only from the abstract point of view of science; it can not be lived, it can not even be represented. The triangle which I trace on the blackboard so as to help me in abstract reasoning is necessarily to the right of the circle tangent to one of its sides, necessarily to the extent that it *is* on the blackboard. And my effort is to surpass the concrete characteristics of the figure traced in chalk by not including its relation to me in my calculations any more than the thickness of the lines or the imperfection of the drawing.

Thus by the mere fact that *there is* a world, this world can not exist without a univocal orientation in relation to me. Idealism has rightly insisted on the fact that relation makes the world. But since idealism took its position on the ground of Newtonian science, it conceived this relation as a relation of reciprocity. Thus it attained only abstract concepts of pure exteriority, of action and reaction, *etc.*, and due to this very fact it missed the world and succeeded only in making explicit the limiting concept of absolute objectivity. This concept in short amounted to that of a *"desert world"* or of "a world without men;" that is, to a contradiction, since it is through human reality that there is a world. Thus the concept of objectivity, which aimed at replacing the in-itself of dogmatic truth by a pure relation of reciprocal agreement between representations, is self-destructive if pushed to the limit.

Moreover the progress of science has led to rejecting this

notion of absolute objectivity. What Broglie is led to call "experience" is a system of univocal relations from which the observer is not excluded. If microphysics can reintegrate the observer into the heart of the scientific system, this is not by virtue of pure subjectivity—this notion would have no more meaning than that of pure objectivity—but as an original relation to the world, as a place, as that toward which all envisaged relations are oriented. Thus, for example, Heysenberg's principle of indeterminacy can not be considered either as an invalidation or a validation of the determinist postulate. Instead of being a pure connection between things, it includes within itself the original relation of man to things and his place in the world. This is sufficiently demonstrated, for example, by the fact that we cannot make the dimensions of bodies in motion increase in proportionate quantities without changing their relative speed. If I examine the movement of one body toward another first with the naked eye and then with the microscope, it will appear to me a hundred times faster in the second case; for although the body in motion approaches no closer to the body toward which it is moving, it has in the same time traversed a space a hundred times as large. Thus the notion of speed no longer means anything unless it is speed in relation to given dimensions of a body in motion. But it is we ourselves who decide these dimensions by our very upsurge into the world and it is very necessary that we decide them, for otherwise they *would not be* at all. Thus they are relative not to the knowledge which we get of them but to our primary engagement at the heart of the world.

   This fact is expressed perfectly by the theory of relativity: an observer placed at the heart of a system can not determine by any experiment whether the system is at rest or in motion. But this relativity is not a "relativism;" it has nothing to do with *knowledge;* better yet, it implies the dogmatic postulate according to which knowledge releases to us *what is.* The relativity of modern science aims at *being.* Man and the world *are* relative beings, and the principle of their being *is* the relation. It follows that the first relation proceeds from human-reality to the world. To come into existence, for me, is to unfold my distances from things and thereby to cause things "to be there." But consequently things are precisely "things-which-exist-at-a-distance-from-me." Thus the world refers to me that univocal relation which is my being and by which I cause it to be revealed.

The point of view of pure knowledge is contradictory; there is only the point of view of *engaged* knowledge. This amounts to saying that knowledge and action are only two abstract aspects of an original, concrete relation. The real space of the world is the space which Lewin calls "hodological." A pure knowledge in fact would be a knowledge without a point of view; therefore a knowledge of the world but on principle located outside the world. But this makes no sense; the knowing being would be only knowledge since he would be defined by his object and since his object would disappear in the total indistinction of reciprocal relations. Thus knowledge can be only an engaged upsurge in a determined point of view which one *is.* For human reality, to be is to-be-there; that is, "there in that chair," "there at that table," "there at the top of that mountain, with these dimensions, this orientation, *etc.*" It is an ontological necessity.

This point must be well understood. For this necessity appears between two contingencies; on the one hand, while it is necessary that I be in the form of being-there, still it is altogether contingent that I be, for I am not the foundation of my being; on the other hand, while it is necessary that I be engaged in this or that point of view, it is contingent that it should be precisely in this view to the exclusion of all others. This twofold contingency which embraces a necessity we have called the *facticity* of the for-itself. We have described it in Part Two. We showed there that the nihilated in-itself, engulfed in the absolute event which is the appearance of the foundation or the upsurge of the for-itself, remains at the heart of the for-itself as its original contingency. Thus the for-itself is supported by a perpetual contingency for which it becomes responsible and which it assimilates without ever being able to suppress it. Nowhere can the for-itself find this contingency anywhere within itself; nor can the for-itself anywhere apprehend and know it—not even by the reflective *cogito*. The for-itself forever surpasses this contingency toward its own possibilities, and it encounters in itself only the nothingness which it has to be. Yet facticity does not cease to haunt the for-itself, and it is facticity which causes me to apprehend myself simultaneously as totally responsible for my being and as totally unjustifiable.

But the world refers to me the image of this unjustifiability in the form of the synthetic unity of its univocal relations to me. It is absolutely necessary that the world appear to me *in order*. And in this sense this order *is me*; it is that image of me which we described in the last chapter of Part Two. But it is wholly contingent that it should be *this* order. Thus it appears as the necessary and totally unjustifiable arrangement of the totality of being. This absolutely necessary and totally unjustifiable order of the things of the world, this order which is myself in so far as I am neither the foundation of my being nor the foundation of a *particular* being— this order is the body as it is on the level of the for-itself. In this sense we could define the body as *the contingent form which is assumed by the necessity of my contingency*. The body is nothing other than the for-itself; it is not an in-itself *in* the for-itself, for in that case it would solidify everything. But it is the fact that the for-itself is not its own foundation, and this fact is expressed by the necessity of existing as an engaged, contingent being among other contingent beings. As such the body is not distinct from the *situation* of the for-itself since for the for-itself, to exist and to be situated are one and the same; on the other hand the body is identified with the whole world inasmuch as the world is the total situation of the for-itself and the measure of its existence.

But a situation is not a pure contingent given. Quite the contrary, it is revealed only to the extent that the for-itself surpasses it toward itself. Consequently the body-for-itself is never a given which I can know. It is there everywhere as the surpassed; it exists only in so far as I escape it by nihilating myself. The body is what I nihilate. It is the in-itself which is surpassed by the nihilating for-itself and which reapprehends the for-itself in this very surpassing. It is the fact that I am my own motivation without being my own foundation, the fact that I am nothing without having to be what I am and yet in so far as I have to be what I am, I am without having to be. In one sense therefore the body is a necessary characteristic of the for-itself; it is not true that the body is the product of an arbitrary decision on the part of a demiurge nor that the union of soul and body is the contingent bringing together of two substances radically distinct. On the contrary, the very nature of the for-itself demands that it be body; that is, that its nihilating escape from being should be made in the form of an engagement in the world. Yet in another sense the body manifests my contingency; we can even say that it is *only* this contingency. The Cartesian rationalists were right in being struck with this characteristic; in fact it represents the individualization of my engagement in the world. And Plato was not wrong either in taking the body as *that which individualizes the soul*.

Yet it would be in vain to suppose that the soul can detach itself from this individualization by separating itself from the body at death or by pure thought, for the soul is the body inasmuch as the for-itself *is* its own individualization.

We shall understand the bearing of these remarks better if we try to apply them to the problem of sense knowledge.

The problem of sense knowledge is raised on the occasion of the appearance in the midst of the world of certain objects which we call the *senses*. First we established that the Other had eyes; later as physiologists dissected cadavers, they learned the structure of these objects; they distinguished the cornea from the crystalline lens and the lens from the retina. They established that the object, crystalline lens, was classed in a family of particular objects—lenses— and that they could apply to the object of their study those laws of geometric optics which concern lenses. More precise dissections effected progressively as surgical instruments were perfected, have taught us that a bundle of nerves leave the retina and end up in the brain. With the microscope we have examined the nerves of cadavers and have determined exactly their trajectory, their point of departure, and their point of arrival. The totality of these pieces of knowledge concerned therefore a certain spatial object called the eye; they implied the existence of space and of the world. In addition they implied that we could see this eye, and touch it; that is, we are ourselves provided with a sensible point of view on things. Finally between our knowledge of the eye and the eve itself are interposed all our technical knowledge (the art of making our scalpels, our lancets) and our scientific skills (e.g., geometric optics, which enables us to construct and use microscopes). In short, between me and the eye which I dissect there is interposed the whole world such as I make it appear by my very upsurge. Later a more thorough examination has enabled us to establish the existence of various nerve endings on the surface of our body. We have even succeeded in acting separately on certain of these endings and performing experiments on living subjects. We then found ourselves in the presence of two objects in the world: on the one hand the stimulant; on the other hand, the sensitive cell or the free nerve ending which we stimulated. The stimulant was a physical-chemical object, an electric current, a mechanical or chemical agent whose properties we knew with precision and which we could vary in intensity or in duration in a definite way. Therefore we were dealing with two mundane objects, and their intra-mundane relation could be established by our own senses or by means of instruments. The knowledge of this relation once again supposed a whole system of scientific and technical skills, in short, the existence of a world and our original upsurge into the world. Our empirical information enabled us, furthermore, to conceive a relation between "the inside" of the Other-as-object and the ensemble of these objective establishments. We learned in fact that by acting on certain senses we "provoked a modification" in the Other's consciousness. We learned this *through language*—that is, through the meaningful and objective reactions of the Other. A physical object (the stimulant), a physiological object (sense), a psychic object (the Other), objective manifestations of meaning (language): such are the terms of the objective relation which we wished to establish. But not one of them could enable us to get out of the world of objects.

On occasion I have served as subject for the research work of physiologists or psychologists. If I volunteered for some experiment of this kind, I found myself suddenly in a laboratory where I perceived a more or less illuminated screen, or else felt tiny electric shocks, or I was brushed by an object which I could not exactly determine but whose global presence I grasped as in the midst of the world and over against me. Not for an instant was I isolated from the world; all these events happened for me in a laboratory in the middle of Paris, in the south building of the Sorbonne. I remained in the Other's presence, and the very meaning of the experiment demanded that I could communicate with him through language. From time to time the experimenter asked me if the screen appeared to me more or less illuminated, if the pressure exerted on my hand seemed to me stronger or weaker, and I replied; that is, I gave objective information concerning things which appeared in the midst of my world. Sometimes an inept experimenter asked me if "my sensation of light was stronger or weaker, more or less intense." Since I was in the midst of objects and in the process of observing these objects, his phrase would have had no meaning for me if I had not long since learned to use the expression "sensation of light" for objective light as it appeared to me in the world at a given instant. I replied therefore that the sensation of light was, for example, less intense, but I meant by this that the screen was *in my opinion* less illuminated. Since I *actually* apprehended the screen as less illuminated, the phrase "in my opinion" corresponded to nothing real except to an attempt not to confuse the objectivity of the world-for-me with a stricter objectivity, which is the result of experimental measures and of the agreement of minds with each other. What I could *know* in each case was a certain object which the experimenter observed during this time and which was my visual organ or certain tactile endings. Therefore the result obtained at the end of the experiment could be only the relating of two series of *objects:* those which were revealed to me during the experiment and those which were revealed during the same period to the experimenter. The illumination of the screen belonged to *my* world; my eyes as objective organs belonged to the world of the experimenter. The connection of these two series was held to be like a bridge between two worlds; under no circumstances could it be a table of correlation between the subjective and the objective. Why indeed should we use the term "subjectivity" for the ensemble of luminous or heavy or odorous objects such as they appeared to me *in this laboratory at Paris on a day in February, etc.* And if despite all we are to consider this ensemble as subjective, then why should we recognize objectivity in the system of objects which were revealed simultaneously to the experimenter, in this laboratory, this same day in February? We do not have two weights or two measures here; we do not encounter anywhere anything which is given as purely *felt,* as experienced for me without objectivation. Here as always I am conscious *of* the world, and on the ground of the world I am conscious *of* certain transcendent objects. As always I surpass what is revealed to me toward the possibility which I have to be—for example, toward that of replying correctly to the experimenter and of enabling the experiment to succeed. Of course these comparisons can give certain objective results: for example, I can establish that the warm water appears cold to me when I put my hand in it after having first plunged my hand in hot water. But this establishment which we pompously call "the law of relativity of sensations" has nothing to do with sensations. Actually we are dealing with a quality of the object which is revealed to me: the warm water *is* cold when I submerge my heated hand in it. A comparison of this objective quality of the water to equally objective information which the thermometer gives me simply reveals to me a contradiction. This contradiction motivates on my part a free choice of true objectivity. I shall give the name subjectivity to the objectivity which I have not chosen. As for the *reasons* for the "relativity of sensations," a further examination will reveal them to me in certain objective, synthetic structures which I shall call *forms* (Gestalt). The Müller-Lyers illusion, the relativity of the senses, *etc.*, are so many names given to objective laws concerning the structures of these forms. These laws teach us nothing about *appearances*, but they concern synthetic structures. I intervene here only to the extent that my upsurge into the world gives birth to this putting *into relation* of objects with each other. As such they are revealed as *forms*. Scientific objectivity consists in considering the structures separately by isolating them from the whole; hence they appear with other characteristics. But in no case do we get out of an existing world. In the same way we might show that what is called the "threshold of sensation" or the specificity of the senses is referred back to pure determinations of objects as such.

Yet some have claimed that this objective relation of the stimulant to the sense organ is itself surpassed toward a relation of the *objective* (stimulant-sense organ) to the subjective (pure sensation) and that this subjective is defined by the action exercised on us by the stimulant through the intermediary of the sense organ. The sense organ appears to us to be affected by the stimulant; the protoplasmic and physical-chemical modifications which appear in the sense organ are not actually produced by that organ; they come to it *from* the outside. At least we assert this in order to remain faithful to the principle of inertia which constitutes all nature as exteriority. Therefore when we establish a correlation between the objective system (stimulant-sensory organ) which we presently perceive, and the subjective system which for us is the ensemble of the internal properties of the other-object, then we are compelled to admit that the new modality which has just appeared in this subjectivity in connection with the stimulation of the sense is also pro-

duced by something other than itself. If it were produced
spontaneously, in fact, it would immediately be cut off from
all connection with the organ stimulated, or if you prefer,
the relation which could be established between them
would be *anything whatsoever*. Therefore we shall conceive
of an objective unity corresponding to even the tiniest and
shortest of perceptible stimulations, and we shall call it sensation. We shall endow this unity with *inertia;* that is, it will
be pure exteriority since, conceived in terms of the *"this,"* it
will participate in the exteriority of the in-itself. This exteriority which is projected into the heart of the sensation
touches it almost in its very existence; its reason for being
and the occasion of its existence are outside of it. It is therefore an *exteriority to itself.* At the same time its *raison d'être*
does not reside in any "internal" fact of the same nature as
it but in a real object (the stimulant) and in the change
which affects another real object (the sense organ). Nevertheless as it remains inconceivable that a certain being existing on a certain level of being and incapable of being
supported in being by itself alone can be determined to
exist by an existent standing on a plane of being which is
radically distinct, I must in order to support the sensation
and in order to furnish it with being, conceive of an environment which is homogeneous with it and constituted
likewise in exteriority. This environment I call *mind* or
sometimes even *consciousness*. But I conceive of this consciousness as an Other's consciousness—that is, as an object. Nonetheless as the relations which I wish to establish
between the sense organ and the sensation must be universal, I posit that the consciousness thus conceived must be
also *my* consciousness, not *for the other* but *in itself*. Thus I
have determined a sort of internal space in which certain
figures called sensations are formed on the occasion of external stimulations. Since this space is pure passivity, I de-

clare that it *suffers* its sensations. But I do not thereby mean only that it is the internal environment which serves as matrix for them. I am inspired at present with a biological vision of the world which I borrow for my objective conception of the sensory organ considered, and I claim that this internal space *lives* its sensation. Thus *life* is a magical connection which I establish between a passive environment and a passive mode of this environment. The mind does not produce its own sensations and hence they remain *exterior* to it; but on the other hand, it appropriates them to itself by living them. The unity of the "lived" and the "living" is no longer indeed a spatial juxtaposition nor a relation of content to container; it is a magical inherence. The mind *is* its own sensations while remaining distinct from them. Thus sensation becomes a particular type of object—inert, passive, and simply lived. Behold us now obliged to bestow on it absolute subjectivity. But the word "subjectivity" must be correctly understood. It does not mean here the belonging to a subject; that is, to a selfness which spontaneously motivates itself. The subjectivity of the psychologist is of an entirely different sort; on the contrary it manifests inertia and the absence of all transcendence. That is subjective which can not get out of itself. And precisely to the extent that sensation, since it is pure exteriority, can be only an impression in the mind, precisely to the extent that it is only itself, only this figure which is formed by an eddy in psychic space, it is not transcendence; it is purely and simply that which is suffered, the simple determination of our receptivity. It is subjectivity because it is neither *presentative* nor *representative*. The subjective quality of the Other-as-object is purely and simply a closed box. Sensation is inside the box.

    Such is the notion of *sensation*. We can see its absurdity. First of all, it is pure fiction. It does not correspond to anything which I experience in myself or with regard to the Other. We have apprehended only the objective universe; all our personal determinations suppose the world and arise as relations to the world. Sensation supposes that man is already in the world since he is provided with sense organs, and it appears in him as the pure cessation of his relations with the world. At the same time this pure "subjectivity" is given as the necessary basis on which all these transcendent relations which its appearance has just caused to disappear will have to be reconstructed. Thus we meet with these three moments of thought:

(1) In order to establish sensation we must proceed on the basis of a certain realism; thus we take as valid our perception of the Other, the Other's senses, and inductive instruments.

(2) But on the level of sensation all this realism disappears; sensation, a modification which one suffers, gives us information only about ourselves; it belongs with the "lived."

(3) Nevertheless it is sensation which I give as the basis of my knowledge or the external world. This basis could not be the foundation of a *real* contact with things; it does not allow us to conceive of an intentional structure of the mind.

We are to use the term *objectivity* not for an immediate connection with being but for certain combinations of sensations which will present more permanence or more regularity or which will accord better with the ensemble of our representations. In particular it is thus that we shall have to define our perception of the Other, the Other's sense organs, and inductive instruments. We are dealing with subjective formations of a particular coherence—that is all. On this level there can be no question of explaining my sensation by the sense organ as I perceive it in the Other or in myself; quite the contrary, it is the sense organ which I explain as a certain association of my sensations. We can see the inevitable circle. My perception of the Other's senses serves me as a foundation for an explanation of sensations and in particular of *my* sensations, but reciprocally my sensations thus conceived constitute the only *reality* of my perception of the Other's senses. In this circle the same object—the Other's sense organ—maintains neither the same nature nor the same truth throughout each of its appearances. It is at first *reality*, and then because it is reality it founds a doctrine which contradicts it. In *appearance* the structure of the classical theory of sensation is exactly that of the Cynic argument of the Liar in that it is precisely because the Cretan tells the truth that he is found to be lying. But in addition, as we have just seen, a sensation is pure subjectivity. How are we supposed to construct an object out of subjectivity? No synthetic grouping can confer an objective quality on what is on principle of the nature of what is lived. If there is to be perception of objects in the world, it is necessary that from the time of our very upsurge we should be in the presence of the world and of objects. Sensation, a hybrid notion between the subjective and the objective, conceived from the standpoint of the object and applied subsequently to the subject, a bastard existence concerning which we can not say whether it exists in fact or in theory—sensation is a pure daydream of the psychologist. It must be deliberately rejected by any serious theory concerning the relations between consciousness and the world.

But if sensation is only a word, what becomes of the senses? No doubt one will recognize that we never in ourselves encounter that phantom and strictly subjective impression which is sensation. One will admit that I apprehend only *the* green of this notebook, of this foliage and never the sensation of green nor even the "quasi-green" which Husserl posits as the hyletic material which the intention animates into green-as-object. One will declare that he is easily convinced of the fact that on the supposition that the phenomenological reduction is possible—which remains to be proved—it will put us face to face with objects put within brackets as the pure correlates of positional acts but not of impressional residues. Nonetheless it is still true that the senses remain. *I* see the green *touch* this cold, polished marble. An accident can deprive me of a whole sense; I can lose my sight, become deaf, *etc.* What then is a sense which does not give us sensation?

The answer is easy. Let us establish first that *senses* are everywhere and yet everywhere inapprehensible. This inkwell on the table is given to me immediately in the form of a *thing,* and yet it is given to me *by sight.* This means that its presence is a visible presence and that I am conscious that it is present to me as visible—that is, I am conscious (of) seeing it. But at the same time that sight is *knowledge* of the inkwell, sight slips away from all knowledge; there is no knowledge of sight. Even reflection will not give us this knowledge. My reflective consciousness will give to me indeed a knowledge of my reflected-on consciousness of the inkwell but not that of a sensory activity. It is in this sense that we must take the famous statement of Auguste Comte: "The eye can not see itself." It would be admissible, indeed, that another organic structure, a contingent arrangement of our visual apparatus would enable a third eye to *see* our two eyes while they were seeing. Can I not see and touch my hand while it is touching? But then I shall be assuming the point of view of the Other with regard to my senses. I should be seeing eyes-as-objects; I can not see the eye seeing; I can not touch my hand *as it is* touching. Thus any sense in so far as it is-for-me is an inapprehensible; it is not the infinite collection of my sensations since I never encounter anything but objects in the world. On the other

hand if I assume a reflective point of view on my consciousness, I shall encounter my consciousness *of* this or that
thing-in-the-world, not my visual or tactile sense; finally if I
can see or touch my sense organs, I have the revelation of
pure objects in the world, not of a revealing or constructive
activity. Nevertheless the senses are there. *There is* sight,
touch, hearing.

On the other hand, if I consider the system of *seen* objects
which appear to me, I establish that they are not presented
to me in just any order; they are *oriented*. Therefore since a
sense can not be defined either by an apprehensible act or
by a succession of lived states, it remains for us to attempt
to define it by its objects. If sight is not the sum of visual
sensations, can it not be the system of seen objects? In this
case it is necessary to return to that idea of *orientation* which
we indicated earlier and to attempt to grasp its significance.

In the first place let us note that orientation is a constitutive structure of the thing. The object appears on the ground
of the world and manifests itself in a relation of exteriority
with other "thises" which have just appeared. Thus its revelation implies the complementary constitution of an undifferentiated ground which is the total perceptive field or the
world. The formal structure of this relation of the figure to
the ground is therefore necessary. In a word, the existence
of a visual or tactile or auditory field is a necessity; silence,
for example, is the resonant field of undifferentiated noises
in which the particular sound on which we focused is swal-
lowed up. But the material connection of a *particular* "this"
to the ground is both chosen and given. It is chosen in so far
as the upsurge of the for-itself is an explicit and internal
negation of a *particular* "this" on the ground of the world: I
look at the cup or the inkwell. It is given in the sense that my
choice operates in terms of an original distribution of the
thises which manifests the very facticity of my upsurge. It is

necessary that the book appear to me on the right *or* on the left side of the table. But it is contingent that the book appears to me specifically on the left, and finally I am free to look at *the book* on the table or at *the table* supporting the book. It is this contingency between the necessity and the freedom of my choice that we call *sense*. It means that an object *must always appear to me all at once*—it is *the cube, the inkwell, the cup* which I see—but that this appearance always takes place in a particular perspective which expresses its relations to the ground of the world and to other *thises*. It is always *the note of the violin* which I hear. But it is necessary that I hear it *through a door* or *by the open window* or *in a concert hall*. Otherwise the object would no longer be in the midst of the world and would no longer be manifested to an existent-rising-up-in-the-world.

On the other hand while it is very true that all the *thises* can not appear at *once* on the ground of the world and that the appearance of certain among them results in the fusion of certain others with the ground, while it is true that each *this* can manifest itself only in one way *at a time* although there exists for it an infinity of ways of appearing, still these rules of appearance should not be considered as subjective and psychological. They are strictly objective and derive from the nature of things. If the inkwell hides a portion of the table from me, this does not stem from the nature of my senses but from the nature of the inkwell and of light. If the object gets smaller when moving away, we must not explain this by some kind of illusion in the observer but by the strictly external laws of perspective. Thus by these objective laws a strictly objective center of reference is defined.

For example, in a perspective scheme the eye is the point toward which all the objective lines converge. Thus the perceptive field refers to a center objectively defined by that reference and located *in the very field* which is oriented around it. Only we do not see this center as the structure of the perceptive field considered; *we are the center*. Thus the order of the objects in the world perpetually refers to us the image of an object which on principle can not be an object *for us* since it is what we have to be. The structure of the world demands that we can not see without *being visible*. The intra-mundane references can be made only to objects in the world, and the seen world perpetually defines a visible object to which its perspectives and its arrangements refer. This object appears in the midst of the world and at the same time as the world. It is always given as an addition to some grouping of objects since it is defined by the orientation of these objects; without it there would be no orientation since all orientations would be equivalent. It is the contingent upsurge of one orientation among the infinite possibilities of orienting the world; it is *this* orientation raised to the absolute. But on this level this object exists for us only in the capacity of an abstract indication; it is what everything indicates to me and what on principle I can not apprehend since it is what I *am*. In fact what I am can not on principle be an object for me inasmuch as I *am it*. The object which the things of the world indicate and which they include in their radius is for itself and on principle a non-object. But the upsurge of my being, by unfolding distances *in terms of a center,* by the very act of this unfolding determines an object which is itself in so far as it causes itself to be indicated by the world; and I could have no intuition of it as object because I am it, I who am presence to myself as the being which is its own nothingness. Thus my being-in-the-world, by the sole fact that it *realizes* a world, causes itself to be indicated to itself as a being-in-the-midst-of-the-world by the world which it realizes. The case could not be otherwise, for my being has no other way of entering into contact with the world except *to be in the world*. It would be impossible for me to realize a world in which I was not and which would be for me a pure object of a surveying contemplation. But on the contrary it is necessary that I lose myself in the world in order for the world to exist and for me to be able to transcend it. Thus to say that I have entered into the world, "come to the world," or that there is a world, or that I have a body is one and the same thing. In this sense my body is everywhere in the world; it is over there in the fact that the lamp-post hides the bush which grows along the path, as well in the fact that the roof up there is above the windows of the sixth floor or in the fact that a passing car swerves from right to left behind the truck or that the woman who is crossing the street appears smaller than the man who is sitting on the sidewalk in front of the café. My body is co-extensive with the world, spread across all things, and at the same time it is condensed into this single point which all things indicate and which I am without being able to know it. This explanation should allow us to understand the meaning of the senses.

A sense is not given *before* sensible objects. For is it not capable indeed of appearing as an object to the Other? Neither is it given *after* sensible objects; for in that case it would be necessary to suppose a world of incommunicable images, simple copies of reality the mechanism of whose appearance was inconceivable. The senses are contemporaneous with objects; they are things "in person" as they are revealed to us in perspective. They represent simply an objective rule of this revelation. Thus sight does not *produce* visual *sensations;* neither is it affected by light rays. It is the collection of all visible objects in so far as their objective and reciprocal relations all refer to certain chosen sizes— submitted to all at once—as measures, and to a certain center of perspective. From this point of view the senses must in no way be identified with subjectivity. In fact all variations which can be registered in a perceptive field are *objective* variations. In particular, the fact that one can cut off vision by "closing the eyelids" is an *external* fact which does not refer to the subjectivity of the apperception. The eyelid, in fact, is merely one object perceived among other objects, an object which hides other objects from me as the result of its objective relation with them. *No longer to see* the objects in my room because I have closed my eyes is *to see* the curtain of my eyelids. In the same way if I put my gloves on the tablecloth, then *no longer to see* a particular design in the cloth is precisely *to see the gloves*. Similarly the *accidents* which affect a sense belong to the province of objects. "I see yellow" because I have jaundice or because I am wearing yellow glasses. In each case the reason for the phenomenon is not found in a subjective modification of the sense nor even in an organic change but in an objective relation between objects in the world; in each case I see "through" something, and the *truth* of my vision is objective. Finally if in one way or another the center of visual reference is destroyed (since destruction can come only from the development of the world according to its own laws—*i.e.*, expressing in a certain way my facticity), visible objects are not by the same stroke annihilated. They continue to exist *for me*, but they exist without any center of reference, as a *visible totality* without the appearance of any particular *this;* that is, they exist in the absolute reciprocity of their relations. Thus it is the upsurge of the for-itself in the world which by the same stroke causes the world to exist as the totality of things and causes senses to exist as the objective mode in which the qualities of things are presented. What is fundamental is my relation to the world, and this relation at once defines the world and the senses according to the point of view which is adopted. Blindness, Daltonism, myopia originally represent *the way in which there is* a world for me; that is, they define my visual sense in so far as this is the facticity of my upsurge. This is why I can know and objectively define my senses but only *emptily*, in terms of the world; all that is necessary is that my rational and universalizing thought should prolong in the abstract the indications which things give to myself about *my* sense and that it *reconstitute* the sense in terms of these signs as the historian reconstitutes an historical personality according to the evidence indicating it. But in this case I have reconstructed the world on the ground of pure rationality by abstracting myself from the world through thought. I survey the world without attaching myself to it; I place myself in an attitude of absolute objectivity, and each sense becomes one object among objects, a center of *relative* reference and one which itself supposes co-ordinates. But thereby I establish in thought the absolute equivalence of all centers of reference. I destroy the world's quality of being a world—without my even being aware of it. Thus the world by perpetually indicating the senses which I am and by inviting me to reconstitute it impels me to eliminate the personal equation which I am by reinstating in the world the center of mundane reference in relation to which the world is arranged. But by the same stroke I escape—through abstract thought—from the senses which I am; that is, I cut my bonds with the world. I place myself in a state of simple surveying, and the world disappears in the absolute equivalence of its infinite possible relations. The senses indeed are our being-in-the-world in so far as we have to be it in the form of being-in-the-midst-of-the-world.

These observations can be generalized; they can be applied *in toto* to *my body* inasmuch as it is the total center of reference which things indicate. In particular our body is not only what has long been called "the seat of the five senses;" it is also the instrument and the end of our actions. It is impossible to distinguish "sensation" from "action" even if we use the terms of classical psychology: this is what we had in mind when we made the observation that reality is presented to us neither as a *thing* nor as an *instrument* but as an instrumental-thing. This is why for our study of the body as a center of action we shall be able to take as a guiding thread the reasoning which has served us to reveal the true nature of the senses.

As soon as we formulate the problem of action, we risk falling into a confusion with grave consequences. When I take this pen and plunge it into the inkwell I am acting. But if I look at Pierre who at that same instant is drawing up a chair to the table, I establish also that he is acting. Thus there is here a very distinct risk of committing the mistake which we denounced *a propos* of the senses; that is, of interpreting *my* action as it *is-for-me* in terms of the Other's action. This is because the only action which I can *know* at the same time that it is taking place is the action of Pierre. I see his gesture and at the same time I determine his goal: he is drawing a chair up to the table *in order to* be able to sit down near the table and to write the letter which he told me he wished to write. Thus I can apprehend all the intermediate positions of the chair and of the body which moves it as instrumental organizations; they are ways to arrive at one pursued end. The Other's body appears to me here as one instrument in the midst of other instruments, not only as a tool to make tools but also as a *tool to manage tools*, in a word as a tool-machine. If I interpret the role of *my* body in relation to *my* action, in the light of the knowledge I have gained of the Other's body, I shall then consider myself as disposing of a certain instrument which I can dispose of at my whim and which in turn will dispose of other instruments all functioning toward a certain end which I pursue.

Thus we are brought back to the classical distinction between the soul and the body; the soul utilizes the tool which is the body. The parallel with the theory of sensation is perfect. We have seen indeed that the latter started from the knowledge of the Other's senses and that subsequently it endowed me with senses exactly similar to the sensible organs which I perceived in the Other. We have seen also the difficulty which such a theory immediately encountered: this is because I then perceive the world and particularly the Other's sense organs through my own sense, a distorting organ, a refracting environment which can give me no information on its own affections. Thus the consequences of the theory ruin the objectivity of the very principle which has served to establish them. The theory of action, since it has an analogous structure, encounters analogous difficulties. In fact if I start with the Other's body, I apprehend it as an instrument and in so far as I myself make use of it as an instrument. I can *utilize it* in order to arrive at ends which I could not attain alone; I *command* its acts through orders or supplications; I can also provoke its act by my own acts. At the same time I must take precautions with respect to a tool which is particularly delicate and dangerous to handle. In relation to it I stand in the complex attitude of the worker with respect to his tool-machine when simultaneously he directs its movements and avoids being caught by it. Once again in order to utilize the Other's body to my best interests I need an instrument which is my own body just as in order to perceive the Other's sense organs I need other sense organs which are my own. Therefore if I conceive of my body in the image of the Other's body, it is an instrument in the world which I must handle delicately and which is like a key to the handling of other tools. But my relations with this privileged instrument can themselves be only technical, and I need an instrument in order to handle this instrument—which refers us to infinity. Thus if I conceive of my sense organs as like those of the Other, they require a sense organ in order to perceive them; and if I apprehend my body as an instrument like the Other's body, it demands an instrument to manage it; and if we refuse to conceive of this appeal to infinity, then we must of necessity admit that paradox of a physical instrument *handled* by a soul, which, as we know, causes us to fall into inextricable aporias.

Let us see whether we can attempt here as with the problem of sensations to restore to the body its nature-for-us. Objects are revealed to us at the heart of a complex of instrumentality in which they occupy a determined *place*. This place is not defined by pure spatial co-ordinates but in relation to axes of practical reference. "*The glass is* on the coffee table;" this means that we must be careful not to upset the glass if we move the table. The package of tobacco *is on* the mantle piece; this means that we must clear a distance of three yards if we want to go from the pipe to the tobacco while avoiding certain obstacles—end tables, footstools, *etc.*—which are placed between the mantle piece and the table. In this sense perception is in no way to be distinguished from the practical organization of existents into a *world*. Each instrument refers to other instruments, to those which are its *keys* and to those for which it is the *key*. But these references could not be grasped by a purely contemplative consciousness. For such a consciousness the hammer would not refer to the nails but would be alongside them; furthermore the expression "alongside" loses all meaning if it does not outline a path which goes from the hammer to the nail and which *must be* cleared. The space which is originally revealed to me is hodological space; it is furrowed with paths and highways; it is instrumental and it is the *location* of tools. Thus the world from the moment of the upsurge of my For-itself is revealed as the indication of acts to be performed; these acts refer to other acts, and those to others, and so on. It is to be noted however that if from this point of view perception and action are indistinguishable, action is nevertheless presented as a future efficacy which surpasses and transcends the pure and simple perceived. Since the perceived is that to which my For-itself is presence, it is revealed to me as co-presence; it is immediate contact, present adherence, it brushes lightly over me. But as such it is offered without my being able *at present* to grasp it. The thing perceived is full of promises; it touches me lightly in passing, and each of the properties which it promises to reveal to me, each surrender silently consented to, each meaningful reference to other objects engages the future.

Thus I am *in the presence* of things which are only promises beyond an ineffable *presence* which I can not possess and which is the pure "being-there" of things; that is, the "mine," my facticity, my body. The cup is there on the saucer; it is presently given to me with its bottom side which *is* there, which everything indicates but which I do not see. And if I wish to see the bottom side—*i.e.*, to make it explicit, to make it "appear-on-the-bottom-of-the-cup"—it is necessary for me to grasp the cup by the handle and turn it upside down. The bottom of the cup is at the end of my projects, and it amounts to the same thing whether I say that the other structures of the cup indicate it as an indispensable element of the cup or that they indicate it to me as the action which will best *appropriate* the cup for me with its meaning. Thus the world as the correlate of the possibilities which I *am* appears from the moment of my upsurge as the enormous skeletal outline of all my possible actions. Perception is naturally surpassed toward action; better yet, it can be revealed only in and through projects of action.

The world is revealed as an "always future hollow," for we are always future to ourselves.[1]

Yet it must be noted that this future of the world which is thus revealed to us is strictly objective. The instrumental-things indicate other instruments or objective ways of making use of them: the nail is "to be pounded in" this way or that, the hammer is "to be held by the handle," the cup is "to be picked up by its handle," *etc.* All these properties of things are immediately revealed, and the Latin gerundives perfectly translate them. Of course they are correlates of non-thetic projects which we are, but they are revealed only as structures of the world: potentialities, absences, instrumentalities. Thus the world appears to me as objectively articulated; it never refers to a creative subjectivity but to an infinity of instrumental complexes.

Nevertheless while each instrument refers to another instrument and this to another, all end up by indicating an instrument which stands as the *key* for all. This center of reference is necessary, for otherwise all the instrumentalities would become equivalent and the world would vanish due to the total undifferentiation of gerundives. Carthage is *"delenda"* for the Romans but *"servanda"* for the Carthaginians. Without relation to its centers Carthage is no longer anything; it falls into the indifference of the in-itself, for the two gerundives annihilate each other. Nevertheless we must of necessity see that the *key* is never *given* to me but only indicated by a sort of gap.[2] What I objectively apprehend in action is a world of instruments which encroach on one another, and each of them as it is apprehended in the very act by which I adapt myself to it and surpass it, refers

---

[1] *"Creux toujours futur."* There is a suggestion here of a mould to be filled but, of course, with no idea of a determined future. Tr.

[2] *Indiquée en creux;* literally, "indicated in a hollow (or mould)." Tr.

to another instrument which must enable me to utilize this one. In this sense the nail refers to the hammer and the hammer refers to the hand and the arm which utilizes it. But it is only to the extent that I cause the nails to be pounded in by the Other that the hand and the arm become in turn instruments which I utilize and which I surpass toward their potentiality. In this case the Other's hand refers me to the instrument which will allow me to utilize this hand (to threats promises-salary, *etc*.). The first term is present everywhere but it is only *indicated*. I do not apprehend *my* hand in the act of writing but only the pen which is writing; this means that I use my pen in order to form letters but not *my hand* in order to hold the pen. I am not in relation to my hand in the same utilizing attitude as I am in relation to the pen; I *am* my hand. That is, my hand is the arresting of references and their ultimate end. The hand is only the utilization of the pen. In this sense the hand is at once the unknowable and non-utilizable term which the last instrument of the series indicates ("book to be read—characters to be formed on the paper—pen") and at the same time the orientation of the entire series (the printed book itself refers back to the hand). But I can apprehend it—at least in so far as it is acting—only as the perpetual, evanescent reference of the whole series. Thus in a duel with swords or with quarter-staffs, it is the quarter-staff which I watch with my eyes and which I handle. In the act of writing it is the point of the pen which I look at in synthetic combination with the line or the square marked on the sheet of paper. But my hand has vanished; it is lost in the complex system of instrumentality in order that this system may exist. It is simply the meaning and the orientation of the system.

Thus, it seems, we find ourselves before a double and contradictory necessity: since every instrument is utilizable

and even apprehensible only by means of another instrument, the universe is an indefinite, objective reference from
tool to tool. In this sense the structure of the world implies
that we can insert ourselves into the field of instrumentality
only by being ourselves an instrument, that we can not *act*
without being *acted on*. Yet on the other hand, an instrumental complex can be revealed only by the determination of a
cardinal meaning of this complex, and this determination is
itself practical and active—to pound a nail, to sow seed. In
this case the very existence of the complex immediately
refers to a center. Thus this center is at once a tool objectively defined by the instrumental field which refers to it
and at the same time the tool which we can not *utilize* since
we should thus be referred to infinity. We do not use this instrument, for we *are it*. It is given to us in no other way than
by the instrumental order of the world, by hodological
space, by the univocal or reciprocal relations of machines,
but it can not be *given* to my action. I do not have to adapt
myself to it nor to adapt another tool to it, but it is my very
adaptation to tools, the adaptation which I am.

This is why if we reject the analogical reconstruction of
my body according to the body of the Other, there remain
two ways of apprehending the body: First, it is *known* and
objectively defined in terms of the world but *emptily*; for
this view it is enough that rationalizing thought reconstitute the instrument which I am from the standpoint of the
indications which are given by the instruments which I utilize. In this case, however the fundamental tool becomes a
relative center of reference which itself supposes other tools
to utilize it. By the same stroke the instrumentality of the
world disappears, for in order to be revealed it needs a reference to an absolute center of instrumentality; the world of
action becomes the world *acted upon* of classical science;
consciousness surveys a universe of exteriority and can no

longer in any way *enter into the world*. Secondly the body is *given concretely* and fully as the very arrangement of things in so far as the For-itself surpasses it towards a new arrangement. In this case the body is present in every action although invisible, for the act reveals the hammer and the nails, the brake and the change of speed, not the foot which brakes or the hand which hammers. The body is *lived* and not *known*. This explains why the famous "sensation of effort" by which Maine de Biran attempted to reply to Hume's challenge is a psychological myth. We never have any sensation of our effort, but neither do we have peripheral sensations from the muscles, bones, tendons, or skin, which have been suggested to replace the sensation of effort. We perceive the *resistance* of things. What I perceive when I want to lift this glass to my mouth is not my effort but the *heaviness of the glass*—that is, its resistance to entering into an instrumental complex which I have made appear in the world.

Bachelard rightly reproaches phenomenology for not sufficiently taking into account what he calls the "coefficient of adversity" in objects.[3] The accusation is just and applies to Heidegger's transcendence as well as to Husserl's intentionality. But we must understand that the instrumentality is primary: it is in relation to an original instrumental complex that things reveal their resistance and their adversity. The bolt is revealed as too big to be screwed into the nut; the pedestal too fragile to support the weight which I want to hold up, the stone too heavy to be lifted up to the top of the wall, *etc*. Other objects will appear as threatening to an instrumental complex already established—the storm and the hail threatening to the harvest, the phyloxera to the vine, the fire to the house. Thus step by step and across the

[3] Bachelard, *L'Eau et les Rêves*, 1942. Editions José Corti.

instrumental complexes already established, their threat will extend to the center of reference which all these instruments indicate, and in turn it will indicate this center through them. In this sense every *means* is simultaneously favorable and adverse but within the limits of the fundamental project realized by the upsurge of the For-itself in the world. Thus my body is indicated originally by instrumental complexes and secondarily by destructive devices. I *live* my body in danger as regards menacing machines as for manageable instruments. My body is everywhere: the bomb which destroys *my* house also damages my body in so far as the house was already an indication of my body. This is why my body always extends across the tool which it utilizes: it is at the end of the cane on which I lean and against the earth; it is at the end of the telescope which shows me the stars; it is on the chair, in the whole house; for it is my adaptation to these tools.

Thus at the end of this account sensation and action are rejoined and become one. We have given up the idea of *first* endowing ourselves with a body in order to study *second* the way in which we apprehend or modify the world through the body. Instead we have laid down as the foundation of the revelation of the body as such our original relation to the world—that is, our very upsurge into the midst of being. Far from the body being first *for us* and revealing things to us, it is the instrumental-things which in their original appearance indicate our body to us. The body is not a screen between things and ourselves; it manifests only the individuality and the contingency of our original relation to instrumental-things. In this sense we defined the senses and the sense organs in general as our being-in-the-world in so far as we have to be it in the form of being-in-the-midst-of-the-world. Similarly we can define *action* as our being-in-the-world in so far as we have to be it in the form of being-an-instrument-in-the-midst-of-the-world. But if I am in the midst of the world, this is because I have caused the world to-be-there by transcending being toward myself. And if I am an instrument in the world, this is because I have caused instruments in general to-be-there by the projection of myself toward my possibles. It is only *in a world* that there can be a body, and a primary relation is indispensible in order that this world may exist. In one sense the body is what I immediately am. In another sense I am separated from it by the infinite density of the world; it is given to me by a reflux of the world toward my facticity, and the condition of this reflux of the world toward my facticity is a perpetual surpassing.

We are now able to define our body's *nature-for-us*. The preceding observations have allowed us to conclude that the body is perpetually the *surpassed*. The body as a sensible center of reference is that *beyond which* I am in so far as I am immediately present to the glass or to the table or to the distant tree which I perceive. Perception, in fact, can be accomplished only at the very place where the object is perceived and *without distance*. But at the same time it unfolds the distances, and that in relation to which the perceived object indicates its distance as an absolute property of its being is the body. Similarly as an instrumental center of instrumental complexes the body can be only the *surpassed;* it is that which I surpass toward a new combination of complexes and which I shall perpetually have to surpass whatever may be the instrumental combination at which I arrive; for every combination from the moment that my surpassing fixes it in its being indicates the body as the center of reference for its own fixed immobility. Thus the body, since it is surpassed, is the Past. It is the immediate presence to the For-itself of "sensible" things in so far as this presence indicates a center of reference and is *already surpassed* either toward the appearance of a new *this* or toward a new combination of instrumental-things. In each project of the For-itself, in each perception the body is there; it is the immediate Past in so far as it still touches on the Present which flees it. This means that it is at once *a point of view and a point of departure*—a point of view, a point of departure which I *am* and which at the same time I surpass toward what I have to be.

This point of view which is perpetually surpassed and which is perpetually reborn at the heart of the surpassing, this point of departure which I do not cease to leave and which is myself remaining behind me—this is the necessity of my contingency. It is doubly necessary. First it is necessary because it is the continual reapprehension of the For-itself by the In-itself and the ontological fact that the For-itself can be only as the being which is not its own foundation. To have a body is to be the foundation of one's own nothingness and not to be the foundation of one's being; I *am* my body to the extent that I *am; I am not* my body to the extent that I am not what I am. It is by my nihilation that I escape it. But I do not thereby make an object of it, for what I am is what I perpetually escape. The body is necessary again as the obstacle to be surpassed in order to be in the world; that is, the obstacle which I am to myself. In this sense it is not different from the absolute order of the world, this order which I cause to arrive in being by surpassing it toward a being-to-come, toward being-beyond-being. We can clearly grasp the unity of these two necessities: being-for-itself is to surpass the world and to cause there to be a world by surpassing it. But to surpass the world is not to survey it but to be engaged in it in order to emerge from it; it is necessary always that a *particular* perspective of surpassing be effected. In this sense *finitude* is the necessary condition of the original project of the For-itself. The necessary condition for me to be what I am not and to not-be what I am—beyond a world which I cause to come into being—this condition is that at the heart of the infinite pursuit which I am there should be perpetually an inapprehensible given. This given which I am without having to be it—except in the mode of non-being—this I can neither grasp nor know, for it is everywhere recovered and surpassed, utilized for my assumed projects. On the other hand everything indicates it to me, every transcendent outlines it in a sort of hollow by its very transcendence without my ever being able to turn back on that which it indicates since I *am* the being indicated. In particular we must not understand the indicated-given as a pure center of reference of a static order of instrumental-things. On the contrary their dynamic order, whether it depends on my action or not, refers to it according to rules, and thereby the center of reference is defined in its change as in its identity. The case could not be otherwise since it is by denying that I am being that I make the world come into being and since it is from the standpoint of my past—*i.e.,* in projecting myself beyond my own being—that I can deny that I am this or that particular being. From this point of view the body—*i.e.,* this inapprehensible given—is a necessary condition of my action. In fact if the ends which I pursue could be attained by a purely arbitrary wish, if it were sufficient to hope in order to obtain, and if definite rules did not determine the use of instruments, I could never distinguish within me desire from will, nor dream from act, nor the possible from the real. No project of myself would be possible since it would be enough to conceive of it in order to realize it. Consequently my being-for-myself would be annihilated in the indistinction of present and future. A phenomenology of action would in fact show that the act supposes a break in continuity between the simple conception and the realization—that is, between a universal and abstract thought such as "A carburetor must not *be clogged*" and a technical and concrete thought directed upon *this* particular carburetor as it appears to me with its absolute dimensions and its absolute position. The condition of this technical thought, which is not distinguished from the act which it directs, is my finitude, my contingency, finally my facticity.

Now, to be exact, I am *in fact* in so far as I have a past, and this immediate past refers to the primary in-itself on the nihilation of which I arise through *birth*. Thus the body as facticity is the past as it refers originally to a *birth;* that is, to the primary nihilation which causes me to arise from the In-itself which I am in fact without having to be it. Birth, the past, contingency, the necessity of a point of view, the factual condition for all possible action on the world—such is the *body,* such it is *for me.* It is therefore in no way a contingent addition to my soul; on the contrary it is a permanent structure of my being and the permanent condition of possibility for my consciousness as consciousness *of* the world and as a transcendent project toward my future. From this point of view we must recognize both that it is altogether contingent and absurd that I am a cripple, the son of a civil servant or of a laborer, irritable and lazy, and that it is nevertheless *necessary* that I be *that* or else something else, French or German or English, *etc.,* a proletarian or bourgeois or aristocrat, *etc.,* weak and sickly or vigorous, irritable or of amiable disposition—precisely because I can not survey the world without the world disappearing. My *birth* as it conditions the way in which objects are revealed to me (objects of luxury or of basic necessity are more or less *accessible,* certain social realities appear to me as *forbidden,* there are barriers and obstacles in my hodological space); *my race* as it is indicated by the Other's attitude with regard to me (these attitudes are revealed as scornful or admiring, as trusting or distrusting); *my class* as it is disclosed by the revelation of the social community to which I belong inasmuch as the places which I frequent refer to it; *my nationality;* my *physiological structure* as instruments imply it by the very way in which they are revealed as resistant or docile and by their very coefficient of adversity; my *character;* my *past,* as everything which I have experienced is indicated as my point of view on the world by the world itself: all this in so far as I surpass it in the synthetic unity of my being in-the-world is *my body* as the necessary condition of the existence of a world and as the contingent realization of this condition.

Now at last we can grasp clearly the definition which we gave earlier of the body in its being-for-us: the body is the contingent form which is taken up by the necessity of my contingency. We can never apprehend this contingency as such in so far as our body is *for us;* for we are a choice, and for us, to be is to choose ourselves. Even this disability from which I suffer I have assumed by the very fact that I live; I surpass it toward my own projects, I make of it the necessary obstacle for my being, and I can not be crippled without choosing myself as crippled. This means that I choose the way in which I constitute my disability (as "unbearable," "humiliating," "to be hidden," "to be revealed to all," "an object of pride," "the justification for my failures," *etc.*). But this inapprehensible body is precisely the necessity that *there be a choice,* that I do not exist *all at once.* In this sense my finitude is the condition of my freedom, for there is no freedom without choice; and in the same way that the body conditions consciousness as pure consciousness of the world, it renders consciousness possible even in its very freedom.

It remains for us to arrive at a conception of what the body is for me; for precisely because the body is inapprehensible, it does not belong to the objects in the world—*i.e.,* to those objects which I know and which I utilize. Yet on the other hand since I can be nothing without being the consciousness of what I am, the body must necessarily be in some way given to my consciousness. In one sense, to be sure, the body is what is indicated by all the instruments which I grasp, and I apprehend the body without knowing it in the very indications which I perceive on the instruments. But if we limit ourselves to this observation, we shall not be able to distinguish, for example, between the body and the telescope through which the astronomer looks at the planets. In fact if we define the body as a contingent point of view on the world, we must recognize that the notion of a point of view supposes a double relation: a relation with the things *on which the body is* a point of view and a relation with the observer *for whom the body is* a point of view. When we are dealing with the body-as-a-point-of-view, this second relation is radically different from the first; it is not truly distinct when we are dealing with a point of view in the world (spectacles, a look-out point, a magnifying glass, *etc.*) which is an objective instrument distinct from the body. A traveler contemplating the landscape *from* a belvedere sees the belvedere as well as the landscape; he sees the trees between the columns of the belvedere, the roof of the belvedere hides the sky from him, *etc.* Nevertheless the "distance" between him and the belvedere is by definition less great than that between his eyes and the panorama. The *point of view* can approach the body to the point of almost being dissolved in it, as we see, for example in the case of glasses, pince-nez, monocles, *etc.*, which become, so to speak, a supplementary sense organ. At its extreme limit—if we conceive of an absolute point of view—the distance between it and the one for whom it is a point of view is annihilated. This means that it would become impossible to withdraw in order to "give oneself plenty of room" and to constitute a new point of view on the point of view. It is precisely this fact, as we have seen, which characterizes the body. It is the instrument which I can not use in the way I use any other instrument, the point of view on which I can no longer take a point of view. This is why on the top of that hill which I call a "good viewpoint," I take a point of view at the very instant when I look at the valley, and this *point of view on the point of view* is my body. But I can not take a point of view on my body without a reference to infinity. Therefore the body can not be *for me* transcendent and known; the spontaneous, unreflective consciousness is no longer the consciousness *of the* body. It would be best to say, using "exist" as a transitive verb—that consciousness *exists* its body. Thus the relation between the body-as-point-of-view and things is an *objective* relation, and the relation of consciousness to the body is an *existential* relation. What do we mean by an existential relation?

First of all, it is evident that consciousness can exist its body only as consciousness. Therefore *my* body is a conscious structure of my consciousness. But precisely because the body is the point of view on which there can not be a point of view, there is on the level of the unreflective consciousness no consciousness *of* the body. The body belongs then to the structures of the non-thetic self-consciousness. Yet can we identify it purely and simply with this non-thetic consciousness? That is not possible either, for non-thetic consciousness is self-consciousness as the free project toward a possibility which is its own; that is, in so far as it is the foundation of its own nothingness. Non-positional consciousness is consciousness (of the) body as being that which it surmounts and nihilates by making itself consciousness—i.e., as being something which consciousness is without having to be it and *which it passes over* in order to be what it has to be. In short, consciousness (of) the body is lateral and retrospective; the body is the *neglected,* the *"passed by in silence."* And yet the body is what this consciousness *is;* it is not even anything except body. The rest is nothingness and silence.

Consciousness of the body is comparable to the consciousness of a *sign.* The sign moreover is on the side of the body; it is one of the essential structures of the body. Now the consciousness of a sign exists, for otherwise we should not be able to understand its meaning. But the sign is that which is *surpassed toward meaning,* that which is neglected for the sake of the meaning, that which is never apprehended for itself, that beyond which the look is perpetually directed. Consciousness (of) the body is a lateral and retrospective consciousness of what consciousness is without having to be it (*i.e.,* of its inapprehensible contingency, of that in terms of which consciousness makes itself a choice) and hence it is a non-thetic consciousness of the manner in which it is *affected.* Consciousness of the body is often confused with original affectivity. Again it is very important to grasp the meaning of this affectivity; and for this we must make a further distinction. Affectivity as introspection reveals it to us is in fact already a *constituted* affectivity; it is consciousness *of* the world. All hate is hate *of* someone; all anger is apprehension of someone as hateful or unjust or faulty; to have sympathy for someone is to "find him sympathetic," *etc.* In these various examples a transcendent "intention" is directed toward the world and apprehends it as such. Already therefore there is a surpassing, an internal negation; we are on the level of transcendence and choice. But Scheler has effectively demonstrated that this "intention" must be distinguished from pure affective qualities. For example, if I have a "headache" I can discover within me an intentional affectivity directed toward my pain so as to "suffer" it, to accept it with resignation, or to reject it, to evaluate it (as unjust, as deserved, as purifying, as humiliat-ing, *etc.*) so as to escape it. Here it is the very intention which is the affection; it is pure act and already a project, a pure consciousness *of* something. This cannot be what we should consider consciousness (of) the body.

In reality this intention can not be the whole of affectivity. Since affectivity is a surpassing, it pre-supposes a sur-passed. Moreover this is proved by the existence of what Baldwin incorrectly calls "emotional abstracts." Baldwin has indeed established that we can realize affectively within us certain emotions without feeling them concretely. For example, if someone tells me of a particular painful event which has just darkened the life of Pierre, I shall ex-claim, "How he must have suffered!" I do not know this suffering and I do not actually *feel* it. These intermediaries between pure knowledge and true affection Baldwin calls "abstracts." But the mechanism of such an abstraction re-mains very obscure. *Who* abstracts? If following M. La-porte's definition we say that to abstract is to think of structures *in isolation* which can not *exist* separately, it is necessary either that we identify emotional abstracts with pure abstract concepts of emotions or else that we recognize that these abstracts can *exist* as such as real modalities of consciousness. In actuality these so-called "emotional ab-stracts" are empty intentions, pure projects of emotion. That is, we direct ourselves towards pain and shame, we strain toward them, consciousness transcends itself—but *emptily.* Grief is there, objective and transcendent, but it lacks concrete existence. It would be better to give to these insubstantial significations the name of affective *images.* Their importance of artistic creation and psychological un-derstanding is undeniable. But the important thing here is the fact that what separates them from real shame, for ex-ample, is the absence of the quality of being *lived.*

There exist therefore pure affective qualities which are surpassed and transcended by affective projects. We shall not make of them as Scheler did, some kind of "hyle" borne upon the flux of consciousness. For us it is simply a matter of the way in which consciousness *exists* its contingency; it is the very texture of consciousness in so far as it surpasses this texture toward its own possibilities; it is the manner in which consciousness *exists* spontaneously and in the non-thetic mode, that which it *constitutes* thetically but implicitly as a point of view on the world. This can be pure grief, but it can also be a mood, an affective, non-thetic tonality, the pure agreeable, the pure disagreeable. In a general way, it is what is called *coenesthesia*. This "coenesthesia" rarely appears without being surpassed toward the world by a transcendent project on the part of the For-itself; as such it can only with difficulty be studied in isolation. Yet there exist some privileged experiences in which it can be apprehended in its purity, in particular what we call "physical" pain. Therefore we shall now examine this experience in order to fix conceptually the structures of the consciousness (of) the body.

My eyes are hurting but I should finish reading a philosophical work this evening. I am reading. The object of my consciousness is the book and across the book the truths which it points out. The body is in no way apprehended for itself; it is a point of view and a point of departure. The words slip by one after the other before me; I *make them slip by;* those at the bottom of the page which I have not yet read still belong to a relative ground or "the-page-as-ground" which is organized upon the "book-as-ground" and on the absolute ground or ground of the world. But from the ground of their indistinction they are calling to me; they already possess the character of a *friable totality;* they are given as "to be made to slip by under my sight." In all this the body is given only *implicitly;* the movement of my eyes belongs only to an observer's glance. For myself I apprehend thetically only this fixed upsurge of the words one after the other. Yet the succession of the words in objective time is given and known through my own temporalization. Their motionless movement is given across a "movement" of my consciousness; and this "movement" of consciousness, a pure metaphor which designates a temporal progression, is for me exactly the movement of my eyes. It is impossible for me to distinguish the movement of my eyes from the synthetic progression of my states of consciousness without resorting to the point of view of the Other. Yet at the very moment that I am reading *my eyes hurt.* Let us note first that this pain can itself be *indicated* by objects of the world; *i.e.,* by the book which I read. It is with more difficulty that the words are detached from the undifferentiated ground which they constitute; they may tremble, quiver; their meaning may be derived only with effort, the sentences which I have just read twice, three times may be given as "not understood," as "to be re-read." But these same indications can be lacking—for example, in the case when my reading "absorbs me" and when I "forget" my pain (which does not mean that it has disappeared since if I happen to gain knowledge of it in a later *reflective* act, it will be given as having always been there). In any case this is not what interests us; we are looking for the way in which consciousness *exists* its pain. But at the start someone will ask, how is the pain given as pain *in the eyes?* Is there not there an intentional reference to a transcendent object, to my body precisely in so far as it exists outside in the world? It is undeniable that pain contains information about itself; it is impossible to confuse pain in the eyes with pain in the finger or the stomach. Nevertheless pain is totally void of intentionality. It must be understood that if pain is given as

pain "in the eyes," there is no mysterious "local sign" there
nor any knowledge either. Pain *is precisely the eyes* in so far
as consciousness "exists them." As such it is distinguished
from other pain by its very existence, not by a criterion nor
by anything added on. To be sure, the expression pain *in the
eyes* supposes a whole constitutive work which we shall
have to describe. But at this stage in the argument, there is
not as yet any reason to consider this, for it is not made.
Pain is not considered from a reflective point of view; it is
not referred back to a body-for-others. It is the-eyes-as-pain
or vision-as-pain; it is not distinguished from my way of
apprehending transcendent words. We ourselves have
called it pain in the eyes for the sake of clarity; but it is not
named in consciousness, for it is not *known*. Pain in the eyes
is distinguished from other possible pains inexpressibly
and by its very being.

This pain however does not exist anywhere among the
actual objects of the universe. It is not to the right or to the
left of the book nor among the truths which are revealed
through the book nor in my body-as-object (the body which
the other sees and which I can always partially touch and
partially see), nor in my body-as-a-point-of-view as the latter is implicitly indicated by the world. Neither must we
say that the pain is an "overprint" or that it is like a har-
mony "superimposed" on the things which I see. Those are
images which have no meaning. Pain then is not in space.
But neither does it belong to objective time; it temporalizes
itself, and it is in and through this temporalization that the
time of the world can appear. What then is this pain?
Simply the translucent matter of consciousness, its *being-
there*, its attachment to the world, in short the peculiar contingency of the act of reading. The pain exists beyond all
attention and all knowledge since it slips into each act of at-

tention and of knowledge, since it is this very act in so far as the act is without being the foundation of its being.

Yet even on this plane of pure being, pain as a contingent attachment to the world can be existed non-thetically by consciousness only if it is surpassed. Pain-consciousness is an internal negation of the world; but at the same time it exists its pain—*i.e.*, itself—as a wrenching away from self. Pure pain as the simple "lived" can not be reached; it belongs to the category of indefinables and indescribables which are what they are. But pain-consciousness is a project toward a further consciousness which would be empty of all pain; that is, to a consciousness whose contexture, whose being-there would be not painful. This *lateral* escape, this wrenching away from self which characterizes pain-consciousness does not for all that constitutes pain as a psychic object. It is a non-thetic project of the For-itself; we apprehend it only through the world. For example, it is given in the way in which the book appears as "about to be read in a hurried, jerky rhythm" where the words press against each other in an infernal, fixed round, where the whole universe is pierced with *anxiety*. In addition—and this is the unique character of corporal existence—the inexpressible which one wishes to flee is rediscovered at the heart of this very wrenching away; it is this which is going to constitute the consciousnesses which surpass it; it is the very contingency and the being of the flight which wishes to flee it. Nowhere else shall we come closer to touching that nihilation of the In-itself by the For-itself and that apprehension of the For-itself by the In-itself which nourishes the very nihilation.

Granted, someone may say. But you are weighting the scales by choosing a case where pain is specifically pain in a functioning organ, pain in the eye while it is looking, in the hand while it is grasping But I can suffer from a wound in my finger while I am reading. In this case it would be difficult to maintain that my pain is the very contingency of my "act of reading."

Let us note first that no matter how absorbed I am in my reading, I do not for all that cease making the world come into being. Better yet, my reading is an act which implies in its very nature the existence of the world as a necessary ground. This certainly does not mean that I have a weaker consciousness of the world but that I am conscious of it *as a ground*. I do not lose sight of the colors, the movements which surround me, I do not cease to hear sounds; they are simply lost in the undifferentiated totality which serves as the background for my reading. Correlatively my body does not cease to be indicated by the world as the total point of view on mundane totality, but it is the world as ground which indicates it. Thus my body does not cease to be *existed* in totality as it is the total contingency of my consciousness. It is what the totality of the world as ground indicates, and at the same time it is the totality which I exist affectively in connection with the objective apprehension of the world. But to the extent that a particular *this* detaches itself as figure on the ground of the world, it correlatively points toward a functional specification of the corporal totality, and by the same stroke my consciousness exists a corporal form which arises on the body-as-totality which it exists. The book is read, and to the extent that I exist and that I surpass the contingency of vision—or if you prefer of reading—*the eyes* appear as figure on the ground of the corporal totality. On this plane of existence the eyes certainly are not the sensory organ seen by the Other but rather the very contexture of my consciousness of seeing inasmuch as this consciousness is a structure of my larger consciousness of the world. To be conscious is always to be conscious of the world, and the world and body are always present to my consciousness although in different ways. But this total consciousness of the world is consciousness of the world as ground for a particular *this;* thus just as consciousness specifies itself in its very act of nihilation, there is the presence of a particular structure of the body on the total ground of corporeality. When I am in the process of reading, I do not cease to be a body seated in a particular arm chair three yards from the window under given conditions of pressure and temperature. And I do not cease to exist this pain in my left index finger any more than I cease to exist my body in general. However I exist the pain in such a way that it disappears in the ground of corporeality as a structure subordinated to the corporal totality. The pain is neither absent nor unconscious; it simply forms a part of that distance-less existence of positional consciousness for itself. If a little later I turn the pages of the book, the pain in my finger, without becoming thereby an object of knowledge, will pass to the rank of existed contingency as a figure on a new organization of my body as the total ground of contingency. Moreover these statements are in agreement with the empirical observation that this is because it is easier when reading to "be distracted" from a pain in the finger or in the lower back then from pain in the eyes. For pain in the eyes *is precisely my reading,* and the words which I read refer me to it every instant, whereas the pain in my finger or back is the apprehension of the world as ground and hence is itself lost as a partial structure in the body as the fundamental apprehension of the ground of the world.

But now suppose that I suddenly cease to read and am at present absorbed in *apprehending* my pain. This means that I direct a reflective consciousness on my present consciousness or consciousness-as-vision. Thus the actual texture of my consciousness reflected-on—in particular my pain—is apprehended and *posited* by my reflective consciousness. We must recall here what we said concerning reflection: it is a total grasp without a point of view; it is a knowledge which overflows itself and which tends to be objectivized, to project the known at a distance so as to be able to contemplate it and to think it. The first movement of reflection is therefore to transcend the pure quality of consciousness in pain toward a pain-as-object. Thus if we restrict ourselves to what we have called an accessory reflection, reflection tends to make of pain something *psychic*.

The psychic object apprehended through pain is *illness*.[4] This object has all the characteristics of pain, but it is transcendent and passive. It is a reality which has its own time, not the time of the external universe nor that of consciousness, but psychic time. The psychic object can then support evaluations and various determinations. As such it is distinct even from consciousness and appears through it; it remains permanent while consciousness develops, and it is this very permanence which is the condition of the opacity and the passivity of illness. But on the other hand, this illness in so far as it is apprehended through consciousness has all the characteristics of unity, interiority, and spontaneity which consciousness possesses—but in degraded form. This degradation confers psychic individuality upon it. That is, first of all, the illness has an absolute cohesion without parts. In addition it has its own duration since it is outside consciousness and possesses a past and a future. But this duration which is only the projection of the original temporalization, is a multiplicity of interpenetration. The illness is "penetrating," "caressing," *etc.* And these charac-

----

[4] In this passage the reader should bear in mind that Sartre uses the word *mal*, which can refer both to a specific disease or to evil in general. Both ideas are involved in his discussion. Tr.

teristics aim only at rendering the way in which this illness is outlined in duration; they are melodic qualities. A pain which is given in twinges followed by lulls is not apprehended by reflection as the pure alteration of painful and non-painful consciousnesses. For organizing reflection the brief respites *are a part* of the illness just as silences are a part of a melody. The ensemble constitutes the *rhythm* and the *behavior* of the illness. But at the same time that it is a passive object, illness as it is seen through an absolute spontaneity which is consciousness, is a projection of this spontaneity into the In-itself. As a passive spontaneity it is magical; it is given as extending itself, as entirely the master of its temporal form. It appears and disappears differently than spatial-temporal objects. If I no longer see the table, this is because I have turned my head, but if I no longer feel my illness, it is because it "has left." In fact there is produced here a phenomenon analogous to that which psychologists of form call the stroboscopic illusion. The disappearance of the illness by frustrating the projects of the reflective for-itself is given as a movement of withdrawal, almost as will. There is an animism of illness; it is given as a living thing which has its form, its own duration, its habits. The sick maintain sort of intimacy with it. When it appears, it is not as a new phenomenon; it is, the sick man will say, "my afternoon crisis." Thus reflection does not join together the moments of the same crisis, but passing over an entire day it links the crises together. Nevertheless this synthesis of recognition has a special character; it does not aim at constituting an object which would remain existing even when it would not be given to consciousness (in the manner of a hate which remains "dormant" or stays "in the unconscious"). In fact when the illness goes away it disappears for good. "Nothing is left of it." But the curious consequence follows that when the illness reappears, it rises up in its very passivity by a sort of spontaneous generation. For example, one can feel its "gentle overtures." It is "coming back again." "This is it." Thus the first pains just like the rest are not apprehended for themselves as a simple, bare texture of the consciousness reflected-on; they are the "announcements" of the illness or rather the illness itself which is born slowly—like a locomotive which gradually gets under way. On the other hand it is very necessary to understand that I constitute the illness *with* the pain. This does not mean that I apprehend the illness as the cause of the pain but rather that each concrete pain is like a note in a melody: it is at once the whole melody and a "moment" in the melody. Across each pain I apprehend the entire illness and yet it transcends them all, for it is the synthetic totality of all the pains, the theme which is developed by them and through them. But the matter of the illness does not resemble that of a melody. In the first place it is something purely lived; there is no distance between the consciousness reflected-on and the pain nor between the reflective consciousness and the consciousness reflected-on. The result is that the illness is transcendent but without distance. It is outside my consciousness as a synthetic totality and already close to being *elsewhere*. But on the other hand it is in my consciousness, it fastens on to consciousness with all its teeth, penetrates consciousness with all its notes; and *these teeth, these notes are my consciousness.*

What has become of *the body* on this level? There has been, we noted, a sort of scission from the moment of the reflective projection: for the unreflective consciousness pain was the body; for the reflective consciousness the illness is distinct from the body, it has its own form, it comes and goes. On the reflective level where we are taking our position—*i.e.*, before the intervention of the for-others—the body is not explicitly and thematically given to consciousness. The reflective consciousness is consciousness *of* the illness. However while the illness has a form which is peculiar to it and a melodic rhythm which confers on it a transcending individuality, it adheres to the for-itself by means of its matter since it is revealed through the pain and as the unity of all my pains of the same type. The illness is *mine* in this sense that I give to it its matter. I apprehend it as sustained and nourished by a certain passive environment in which the passivity is precisely the projection into the in-itself of the contingent facticity of the pains. It is *my* passivity. This passive environment is not apprehended for itself except as the matter of the statue is apprehended when I perceive its form, and yet it is there. *The illness feeds on this passivity* and magically derives new strength from it just as Antaeus was nourished by the earth. It is my body on a new plane of existence; that is, as the pure noematic correlate of a reflective consciousness. We shall call it a *psychic body*. It is not yet *known* in any way, for the reflection which seeks to apprehend the pain-consciousness is not yet cognitive. This consciousness is affectivity in its original upsurge. It apprehends the illness as an object but as an affective object. One directs oneself first toward one's pain so as to hate it, to endure it with patience, to apprehend it as unbearable, sometimes to love it, to rejoice in it (if it foretells a release, a cure), to evaluate it in some way. Naturally it is the illness which is evaluated or rather which rises up as the necessary correlate of the evaluation. The illness is therefore not known; it is *suffered,* and similarly the body is revealed by the illness and is likewise suffered by consciousness. In order to add cognitive structures to the body as it has been given to reflection, we will have to resort to the Other. We can not discuss this point at present, for it is necessary first to bring to light the structures of the body-for-others.

At present, however, we can note that this psychic body

since it is the projection on the plane of the in-itself of the intra-contexture of consciousness, provides the implicit matter of *all* the phenomena of the psyche. Just as the original body was existed by each consciousness as its own contingency, so the psychic body is *suffered* as the contingency of hate or of love, of acts and qualities, but this contingency has a new character. In so far as it was existed by consciousness it was the recapture of consciousness by the in-itself; in so far as it is suffered by reflection *in* the illness or the hate or the enterprise, it is *projected into* the in-itself. Hence it represents the tendency of each psychic object beyond its magical cohesion to be parcelled out in exteriority; it represents beyond the magical relations which unite psychic objects to each other, the tendency of each one of them to be isolated in an insularity of indifference. It is therefore a sort of implicit space supporting the melodic duration of the psychic. In so far as the body is the contingent and indifferent matter of all our psychic events, the body determines a *psychic space*. This space has neither high nor low, neither left nor right; it is without parts in as much as the magical cohesion of the psychic comes to combat its tendency towards a division in indifference. This is nonetheless a *real* characteristic of the *psyche*—not that the psyche is *united* to a body but that under its melodic organization the body is its substance and its perpetual condition of possibility. It is this which appears as soon as we *name* the psychic. It is this which is at the basis of the mechanistic and chemical metaphors which we use to classify and to explain the events of the psyche. It is this which we aim at and which we form into images (image-making consciousnesses) which we produce in order to aim at absent feelings and make them present. It is this, finally, which motivates and to some degree justifies psychological theories like that of the unconscious, problems like that of the preservation of memories.

It goes without saying that we have chosen physical pain for the sake of an example and that there are thousands of other ways, themselves contingent, to exist our contingency. In particular we must note that when no pain, no specific satisfaction or dissatisfaction is "existed" by consciousness, the for-itself does not thereby cease to project itself beyond a contingency which is pure and so to speak unqualified. Consciousness does not cease "to have" a body. Coenesthetic affectivity is then a pure, nonpositional apprehension of a contingency without color, a pure apprehension of the self as a factual existence. This perpetual apprehension on the part of my for-itself of an *insipid* taste which I cannot place, which accompanies me even in my efforts to get away from it, and which is *my* taste—this is what we have described elsewhere under the name of *Nausea*. A dull and inescapable nausea perpetually reveals my body to my consciousness. Sometimes we look for the pleasant or for physical pain to free ourselves from this nausea; but as soon as the pain and the pleasure are existed by consciousness, they in turn manifest its facticity and its contingency; and it is on the ground of this nausea that they are revealed. We must not take the term *nausea* as a metaphor derived from our physiological disgust. On the contrary, we must realize that it is on the foundation of this nausea that all concrete and empirical nauseas (nausea caused by spoiled meat, fresh blood, excrement, *etc.*) are produced and make us vomit.

II. THE BODY-FOR-OTHERS

WE have just described the being of my body *for-me*. On this ontological plane my body is such as we have described it and it *is only that*. It would be useless to look there for traces of a physiological organ, of an anatomical and spatial constitution. Either it is the center of reference indicated emptily by the instrumental-objects of the world or else it is the *contingency which the for-itself exists*. More exactly, these two modes of being are complementary. But the body knows the same avatars as the for-itself; it has other planes of existence. It exists also *for-others*. We must now study it in this new ontological perspective. To study the way in which my body appears to the Other or the way in which the Other's body appears to me amounts to the same thing. In fact we have established that the structures of my being-for-the-Other are identical to those of the Other's being-for-me. It is then in terms of the Other's being-for-me that—for the sake of convenience—we shall establish the nature of the body-for-others (that is, of the Other's body).

We showed in the preceding chapter that the body is not that which first manifests the Other to me. In fact if the fundamental relation of my being to that of the Other were reduced to the relation of my body to the Other's body, it would be a purely external relation. But my connection with the Other is inconceivable if it is not an internal negation. I must apprehend the Other first as the one for whom I exist as an object; the reapprehension of my selfness causes the Other to appear as an object in a second moment of prehistoric historization. The appearance of the Other's body is not therefore the primary encounter; on the contrary, it is only one episode in my relations with the Other and in particular in what we have described as making an object of the Other. Or if you prefer, the Other exists for me first and I apprehend him in his body *subsequently*. The Other's body is for me a secondary structure.

In the fundamental phenomenon of making an object of the Other, he appears to me as a transcendence-transcended. That is, by the mere fact that I project myself toward my possibilities, I surpass and transcend the Other's transcendence. It is put out of play; it is a transcendence-as-object. I apprehend this transcendence in the world, and originally, as a certain arrangement of the instrumental-things of *my* world inasmuch as they indicate *in addition* a secondary center of reference which is in the midst of the world and which is not me. These indications—unlike the indications which *indicate* me—are not constitutive of the indicating thing; they are lateral properties of the object. The Other, as we have seen, can not be a constitutive concept of the world. These indications all have therefore an original contingency and the character of an *event*. But the center of reference which they indicate is indeed *the Other* as a transcendence simply contemplated or transcended. The secondary arrangement of objects refers me to the Other as to the organizer or to the beneficiary of this arrangement, in short to an instrument which disposes of instruments in view of an end which it itself produces. But in turn I surpass this end and utilize it; it is in the midst of the world and I can make use of it for my own ends. Thus the Other is at first indicated by things as an instrument. Things also indicate me too as an instrument, and I am a body precisely in so far as I make myself be indicated by things. Therefore it is the Other-as-body whom things indicate by their lateral and secondary arrangements. The fact is that I actually do not know instruments which do not refer secondarily to the Other's body.

Earlier we pointed out that I could not take any point of view on my body in so far as it was designated by things. The body is, in fact, the point of view on which I can take no point of view, the instrument which I can not utilize in the way I utilize any other instrument. When by means of universalizing thought I tried to think of my body emptily as a pure instrument in the midst of the world, the immediate result was the collapse of the world as such. On the other hand, because of the mere fact that *I am not the Other,* his body appears to me originally as a point of view on which I can take a point of view, an instrument which I can utilize with other instruments. The Other's body is indicated by the round of instrumental-things, but in turn it indicates other objects; finally it is integrated with *my* world, and it indicates *my body.* Thus the Other's body is radically different from my body-for-me; it is the tool which I am not and which I utilize (or which resists me, which amounts to the same thing). It is presented to me originally with a certain objective coefficient of utility and of adversity. The Other's body is therefore the Other himself as a transcendence-instrument.

These same remarks apply to the Other's body as the synthetic ensemble of sense organs. We do not *discover* in and through the Other's body the possibility which the Other has of knowing us. This is revealed fundamentally in and through my *being-as-object for the Other;* that is, it is the essential structure of our original relation with the Other. And in this original relation the flight of *my* world toward the Other is equally given. By the reapprehension of my selfness I transcend the Other's transcendence inasmuch as this transcendence is the permanent possibility of apprehending myself as an object. Due to this fact it becomes a purely given transcendence surpassed toward my own goals, a transcendence which simply "is-there," and the knowledge which the Other has of me and of the world becomes knowledge-as-an-object. This means that it is a given property of the Other, a property which in turn I can *know.* In truth this knowledge which I get of it remains empty in this sense that I shall never know *the act of knowing;* this act, since it is pure transcendence can be apprehended only by itself in the form of non-thetic consciousness or by the reflection issuing from it. What I know is only knowledge as *being-there* or, if you like, *the being-there of knowledge*. Thus this relativity of the sensory organ which is revealed to my universalizing reason but which can not be thought, so far as my own sense is concerned, without determining the collapse of the world—this I apprehend *first* when I apprehend the Other-as-object. I apprehend it *without danger;* for since the Other forms part of my universe, his relativity can not determine the collapse of this universe. The senses of the Other are *senses known as knowing.*

We can see here the explanation of the error of psychologists who define *my senses* by the Other's senses and who give to the sense organ as it is for me a relativity which belongs to its being-for-others. We can see also how this error becomes truth if we place it on its proper level of being after we have determined the true order of being and of knowing. Thus the objects of my world indicate laterally an object-center-of-reference which is the Other. But this center in turn appears to me from a point-of-view-without-a-point-of-view which is mine, which is my body or my contingency. In short, to employ an inaccurate but common expression, *I know the Other through the senses.* Just as the Other is the instrument which I utilize in the manner of the instrument which I am and which no instrument can any longer utilize, so he is the ensemble of sense organs which are revealed to my *sense knowledge;* that is, he is a facticity which appears to a facticity. Thus there can be in its true place in the order of knowing and of being, a study of the Other's sense organs as they are known through the senses by me. This study will attach the greatest importance to the function of these sense organs—*which is to know.* But this knowledge in turn will be a pure object for me; here, for example, belongs the false problem of "inverted vision." In reality the sensory organ of the Other originally is in no way an instrument of knowledge for him; it is simply the

Other's knowledge, his pure act of knowing in so far as this knowledge exists in the mode of an object in *my* universe.

Nevertheless we have as yet defined the Other's body only in so far as it is indicated laterally by the instrumental-things of my universe. Actually this by no means gives us his being-there in "flesh and blood." To be sure, the Other's body is everywhere present in the very indication which instrumental-things give of it since they are revealed as utilized by him and as known by him. This room in which I wait for the master of the house reveals to me in its totality the body of its owner: this easy chair is a chair-where-he-sits, this desk is a desk-at-which-he-writes, this window is a window through which there enters the light-which-illuminates-the-objects-which-he-sees. Thus it is an outline complete with all its parts, and this outline is an outline-of-an-object; an object can come at every instant to fill the outline with content. But still the master of the house "is not there." He is *elsewhere*; he is *absent*.

Now we have seen that absence is a structure of *being-there*. To be absent is to-be-elsewhere-in-my-world; it is to be already given for me. As soon as I receive a letter from my cousin in Africa, his being-elsewhere is concretely given to me by the very indications of this letter, and this being-elsewhere is a being-somewhere; it is already his body. We can in no other way explain why a mere letter from a beloved woman sensually affects her lover; all the body of the beloved is present as an absence in these lines and on this paper. But since the being-elsewhere is a *being-there* in relation to a concrete ensemble of instrumental-things in a *concrete situation*, it is already facticity and contingency. It is not only the *encounter* which I had yesterday with Pierre which defines his contingency and mine; his absence yesterday similarly defined our contingencies and our facticities. And this facticity of the absent is implicitly given in these instrumental-things which indicate it; his abrupt appearance does not add anything. Thus the Other's body is his *facticity* as an instrument and as a synthesis of sense organs as it is revealed to my facticity. It is given to me as soon as the Other exists for me in the world; the presence or absence of the Other changes nothing.

But look! Now Pierre appears. He is entering my room. This appearance changes nothing in the fundamental structure of my relation to him; it is contingency but so was his absence contingency. Objects indicate him to me: the door which he pushes indicates a human presence when it opens before him, the same with the chair when he sits down, *etc.*

But the objects did not cease to indicate him during his absence. Of course I exist for him, he speaks to me. But I existed equally yesterday when he sent me that telegram, which is now on my table, to tell me of his coming. Yet there is something new. This is the fact that he appears at present on the ground of the world as a *this* which I can look at, apprehend, and utilize directly. What does this mean? First of all, the facticity of the Other—that is, the contingency of his being—is now *explicit* instead of being implicitly contained in the lateral indications of instrumental-things. This facticity is precisely what the Other *exists*—in and through his for-itself; it is what the other perpetually lives in nausea as a nonpositional apprehension of a contingency which he is, as a pure apprehension of self as a factual existence. In a word, it is his *coenesthesia*. The Other's appearance is the revelation of the taste of his being as an immediate existence. I, however, do not grasp this taste as he does. Nausea for him is not knowledge; it is the non-thetic apprehension of the contingency which he *is*. It is the surpassing of this contingency toward the unique possibilities of the for-itself. It is an existed contingency, a contingency submitted to and refused. It is this same contingency, and no other, which I

presently grasp. But I *am not* this contingency. I surpass
it toward my own possibilities, but this surpassing is the
transcendence *of an Other*. It is given to me in entirety and
without appeal; it is irremediable. The Other's for-itself
wrenches itself away from this contingency and perpetually
surpasses it. But in so far as I transcend the Other's transcendence, I fix it. It is no longer a resource against facticity;
quite the contrary, it participates in turn in facticity, it em-
anates from facticity. Thus nothing comes to interpose itself
between the Other's pure contingency as a *taste for himself*
and my consciousness. Indeed I apprehend *this* taste as it is
existed. However, from the very fact of my otherness, this
taste appears as a known and given *this* in the midst of the
world. This body of the Other is given to me as the pure in-
itself of his being—an in-itself among in-itselfs and one
which I surpass toward my possibilities. This body of the
Other is revealed therefore with two equally contingent
characteristics: it is here and could be elsewhere; that is,
instrumental-things could be arranged otherwise in relation to it, could indicate it otherwise; the distance between
the chair and this body could be different; the body is like
this and could be otherwise—*i.e.*, I grasp its original contingency in the form of an objective and contingent configura-
tion. But in reality these two characteristics are only one.
The second only makes the first present, only makes it explicit for me. This body of the Other is the pure fact of the
Other's presence in *my* world as a being-there which is
expressed by a being-as-this. Thus the Other's very existence as the Other-for-me implies that he is revealed as a
tool possessing the property of knowing and that this property of knowing is bound to some objective existence. This
is what we shall call the necessity for the Other to be contingent for me.

From the moment that *there is* an Other, it must be concluded that he is an instrument provided with certain sense organs. But these considerations only serve to show the abstract necessity for the Other to have a body. This body of the Other as I encounter it is the revelation as object-for-me of the contingent form assumed by the necessity of this contingency. Every Other must have sense organs but not necessarily *these* sense organs, not *any particular face* and finally not *this face*. But face, sense organs, presence—all that is nothing but the contingent form of the Other's necessity to *exist himself* as belonging to a race, a class, an environment, *etc.*, in so far as this contingent form is surpassed by a transcendence *which does not have to exist it*. What for the Other is his *taste of himself* becomes for me the *Other's flesh*. The flesh is the pure contingency of presence. It is ordinarily hidden by clothes, make-up, the cut of the hair or beard, the expression, *etc.* But in the course of long acquaintance with a person there always comes an instant when all these disguises are thrown off and when I find myself in the presence of the pure *contingency of his presence*. In this case I achieve in the face or the other parts of a body the pure intuition of the flesh. This intuition is not only knowledge; it is the affective apprehension of an absolute contingency, and this apprehension is a particular type of *nausea*.

The Other's body is then the facticity of transcendence transcended as it refers to my facticity. I never apprehend the Other as body without at the same time in a non-explicit manner apprehending my body as the center of reference indicated by the Other. But all the same we can not perceive the Other's body *as flesh*, as if it were an isolated object having purely external relations with other thises. That is true only for a *corpse*. The Other's body as flesh is immediately given as the center of reference in a situation which is synthetically organized around it, and it is inseparable from this situation. Therefore we should not ask how the Other's body can be first body for me and subsequently enter into a situation. The Other is originally given to me as a *body in situation*. Therefore there is not, for example, first a body and later action. But the body is the objective contingency of the Other's action. Thus once again we find on another plane an ontological necessity which we pointed out in connection with the existence of my body for me: the contingency of the for-itself, we said, can be existed only in and through a transcendence; it is the reapprehension—perpetually surpassed and perpetually reapprehending—of the for-itself, the reapprehension of the for-itself by the in-itself on the ground of the primary nihilation. Similarly here the Other's body as flesh can not *be inserted* into a situation preliminarily defined. The Other's body is precisely that in terms of which there is a situation. Here also it can exist only in and through a transcendence. Now, however, this transcendence is at the start transcended; it is itself an object. Thus Pierre's body is not first a hand which could subsequently take hold of this glass; such a conception would tend to put the corpse at the origin of the living body. But his body is the complex hand-glass, since the *flesh* of the hand marks the original contingency of this complex.

Far from the relation of the body to objects being a problem, we never apprehend the body outside this relation. Thus the Other's body is *meaningful*. Meaning is nothing other than a fixed movement of transcendence. A body is a body as this mass of flesh which it *is* is defined by the table which the body looks at, the chair in which it sits, the pavement on which it walks, *etc*. But to proceed further, there could be no question of exhausting the meanings which constitute the body—by means of reference to concerted actions, to the rational utilization of instrumental-complexes. The body is the totality of meaningful relations to the world. In this sense it is defined also by reference to the air which it breathes, to the water which it drinks, to the food which it eats. The body in fact could not appear without sustaining meaningful relations with the totality of what is. Like *action, life* is a transcended transcendence and a meaning. There is no difference in nature between action and life conceived as a totality. Life represents the ensemble of meanings which are transcended toward objects which are not posited as *thises* on the ground of the world. *Life* is the Other's body-as-ground in contrast to the body-as-figure inasmuch as this body-as-ground can be apprehended, not by the Other's for-itself and as something implicit and non-positional, but precisely, explicitly, and objectively *by me.* His body appears then as a meaningful figure on the ground of the universe but without ceasing to be a ground for the Other and precisely *as a ground.* But here we should make an important distinction: the Other's body actually appears "to my body." This means that there is a facticity in my point of view on the Other. In this sense we must not confuse my possibility of apprehending an organ (an arm, a hand) on the ground of the corporal totality and, on the other hand, my explicit apprehension of the Other's body or of certain structures of this body in so far as they are lived by the Other as the *body-as-ground.* It is only in the second case that we apprehend the Other as *life.* In the first instance it can happen that we apprehend as ground that which is figure for him. When I look at his hand, the rest of his body is united into ground. But it is perhaps his forehead or his thorax which for him exists non-thetically as figure on a ground in which his arms and his hands are dissolved.

The result, of course, is that the being of the Other's body is for me a synthetic totality. This means: (1) I can never apprehend the Other's body except in terms of a total situation which indicates it. (2) I can not perceive any organ of the Other's body in isolation, and I always cause each single organ to be indicated to me in terms of the totality of the *flesh* or of *life*. Thus my perception of the Other's body is radically different from my perception of things.

(1) The other moves within limits which appear in immediate connection with his movements and which are the terms within which I cause the meaning of these movements to be indicated to myself. These limits are both spatial and temporal. Spatially it is the glass placed *at a distance* from Pierre which is the meaning of his actual gesture. Thus in my perception of the ensemble "table-glass-bottle, *etc.*," I go to the movement of the arm in order to make known to myself what it is. If the arm is visible and if the glass is hidden, I perceive Pierre's movement in terms of the pure idea of *situation* and in terms of the goal aimed at emptily beyond the objects which hide the glass from me, and this is the meaning of the gesture.

Pierre's gesture which is revealed to me in the present I always apprehend temporally from the standpoint of the future goals toward which he is reaching. Thus I make known to myself the present of the body by means of its future and still more generally, by means of the future of the world. We shall never be able to understand anything about the psychological problem of the perception of the Other's body if we do not grasp first this essential truth—that the Other's body is perceived wholly differently than other bodies: for in order to perceive it we always move to it from what is outside of it, in space and in time; we apprehend its gesture "against the current" by a sort of inversion of time and space. To perceive the Other is to make known to oneself what he is by means of the world.

(2) I never perceive an arm raised alongside a motionless body. I perceive Pierre-who-raises-his-hand. This does not mean that by an act of judgment I relate the movement of

the hand to a "consciousness" which instigated it; rather I can apprehend the movement of the hand or of the arm only as a temporal structure of the whole body. Here it is the whole which determines the order and the movement of its parts. In order to prove that we are dealing here with an original perception of the Other's body, we need only recall the horror we feel if we happen to see an arm which looks "as if it did not belong to any body," or we may recall any one of those rapid perceptions in which we see, for example, a hand (the arm of which is hidden) crawl like a spider up the length of the doorway. In such cases there is a disintegration of the body, and this disintegration is apprehended as extraordinary. In addition, we know the positive proofs the Gestalt psychology has often advanced. It comes as a shock when a photograph registers an enormous enlargement of Pierre's hands as he holds them forward (because the camera gasps them in their own dimension and without synthetic connection with the corporal totality), for we perceive that these same hands appear without enlargement if we look at them with the naked eye. In this sense the body appears within the limits of the situation as a synthetic totality of *life* and *action*.

Following these observations, it is evident that Pierre's body is in no way to be distinguished from Pierre-for-me. The Other's body with its various meanings exists only for me: to be an object-for-others or to-be-a-body are two ontological modalities which are strictly equivalent expressions of the being-for-others on the part of the for-itself. Thus the meanings do not refer to a mysterious psychism; they *are* this psychism in so far as it is a transcendence-transcended. Of course there is a psychic cryptography; certain phenomena are "hidden." But this certainly does not mean that the meanings refer to something "beyond the body." They refer to the world and to themselves. In particular these emo-

tional manifestations or, more generally, the phenomena er-
roneously called the phenomena of *expression*, by no means
indicate to us a hidden affection lived by some psychism
which would be the immaterial object of the research of the
psychologist. These frowns, this redness, this stammering,
this slight trembling of the hands, these downcast looks
which seem at once timid and threatening—these do not *ex-
press* anger; they *are* the anger. But this point must be clearly
understood. In itself a clenched fist is nothing and means
nothing. But also we never perceive a *clenched fist*. We perceive a man who in a certain situation clenches his fist. This
meaningful act considered in connection with the past and
with possibles and understood in terms of the synthetic totality "body in situation" *is* the anger. It refers to nothing
other than to actions in the world (to strike, insult, *etc.*); that
is, to new meaningful attitudes of the body. We can not get
away from the fact that the "psychic object" is entirely released to perception and is inconceivable outside corporeal
structures.

If this fact has not been taken into account hitherto or if
those who have supported it, like the Behaviorists, have not
themselves very well understood what they wanted to say
and have shocked the world with their pronouncements,
this is because people too readily believe that all perceptions are of the same kind. Actually perception must release
to us immediately the spatial-temporal object. Its fundamental structure is the internal negation, and it releases to
me the object *as it is,* not as an empty image of some reality
beyond reach. But precisely for this reason a new structure
of perception corresponds to each type of reality. The body
is the psychic object *par excellence—the only psychic object.*
But if we consider that the body is a transcended transcendence, then the perception of it can not *by nature* be of the
same type as that of inanimate objects. We must not under-

stand by this that the perception is progressively enriched but that originally it is of another structure. Thus it is not necessary to resort to habit or reason by analogy in order to explain how we *understand* expressive conduct. This conduct is originally released to perception as understandable; its meaning is part of its being just as the color of the paper is part of the being of the paper. It is therefore no more necessary to refer to other conduct in order to understand a particular conduct than to refer to the color of the table, or of another paper or of foliage in order to perceive the color of the folio which is placed before me.[5]

The Other's body, however, is given to us immediately as what the Other *is*. In this sense we apprehend it as that which is perpetually surpassed toward an end by each particular meaning. Take for example a man who is walking. From the start I understand his walking in terms of a spatial-temporal ensemble (alley-street-sidewalk-shops-cars, *etc.*) in which certain structures represent the meaning-to-come of the walking. I perceive this walking by going from the future to the present—although the future in which there is a question belongs to universal time and is a pure "now" which is not yet. The walking itself, a pure, inapprehensible, and nihilating becoming is the *present*. But this present is a surpassing toward a future goal on the part of *something* which is walking; beyond the pure and inapprehensible present of the movement of the arm we attempt to grasp the substratum of the movement. This substratum, which we never apprehend as it *is* except in the corpse, is yet always there as the surpassed, *the past*. When I speak of an arm-in-motion, I consider this arm which *was at rest* as the substance of the motion. We pointed out in Part Two that such

---

[5] If Sartre did not intend to pun on the words *feuillage* and *feuille*, then I apologize for my feeble attempt with "foliage" and "folio." Tr.

a conception can not be supported. What moves can not be
the motionless arm; motion is a disorder of being. It is
nonetheless true that the psychic movement refers to two
limits—the future terminus of its *result,* and the past terminus—the motionless organ which it alters and surpasses. I
perceive the movement-of-the-arm as a perpetual, inapprehensible reference toward a past-being. This past-being (the
arm, the leg, the whole body at rest) I do not see at all; I can
never catch sight of it except *through* the movement which
surpasses it and to which I am a presence—just as one gets
a glimpse of a pebble at the bottom of the stream through
the movement of the water. Yet this immobility of being
which is always *surpassed and never realized,* to which I perpetually refer in order to say *what is* in motion—this is pure
facticity, pure *flesh,* the pure *in-itself* as the past of a transcended transcendence which is perpetually being made
past.

This pure in-itself, which exists only by virtue of being
surpassed and in and through this surpassing, falls to the
level of the *corpse* if it ceases to be simultaneously revealed
and hidden by the transcendence-transcended. As a *corpse*—
i.e., as the *pure past of a life,* as simply the *remains*—it is still
truly understandable only in terms of the surpassing which
no longer surpasses it: it is *that which has been surpassed toward situations perpetually renewed.* On the other hand, in so
far as it appears at present as a pure in-itself, it exists in relation to other "thises" in the simple relation of indifferent
exteriority: the corpse is *no longer in situation.* At the same
time it collapses into itself in a multiplicity of sustaining beings, each maintaining purely external relations with the
others. The study of exteriority, which always implies facticity since this exteriority is never percepible except on the
corpse, is *anatomy.* The synthetic reconstitution of the living
person from the standpoint of corpses, is *physiology.* From

the outset physiology is condemned to understand nothing of life since it conceives life simply as a particular modality of death, since it sees the infinite divisibility of the corpse as primary, and since it does not know the synthetic unity of the "surpassing towards" for which infinite divisibility is the pure and simple *past*. Even the study of life in the living person, even vivisection, even the study of the life of protoplasm even embryology or the study of the egg can not rediscover life; the organ which is observed is living, but it is not established in the synthetic unity of a *particular* life; it is understood in terms of anatomy—*i.e.*, in terms of death. There is therefore an enormous error in believing that the Other's body, which is originally revealed to us, is the body of anatomical-physiology. The fault here is as serious as that of confusing our senses "for ourselves" with our sensory organs for others. The Other's body is the facticity of the transcendence-transcended as this facticity is perpetually a *birth;* that is, as it refers to the indifferent exteriority of an in-itself perpetually surpassed.

These considerations enable us to explain what is called *character*. It should be noted in fact that character has distinct existence only in the capacity of an object of knowledge for the Other. Consciousness does not know its own character—unless in determining itself reflectively from the standpoint of another's point of view. It exists its character in pure indistinction non-thematically and non-thetically in the proof which it effects of its own contingency and in the nihilation by which it recognizes and surpasses its facticity. This is why pure introspective self-description does not give us character. Proust's hero "does not have" a directly apprehensible character; he is presented first as being conscious of himself as an ensemble of general reactions common to all men ("mechanisms" of passion, emotions, a certain order of memories, *etc.*) in which each man can recognize himself. This is because these reactions belong to the general "nature" of the psychic. If (as Abraham attempted in his book on Proust) we succeed in determining the character of Proust's hero (for example, his weakness, his passivity, his particular way of linking love and money), this is because we are interpreting brute givens. We adopt an external point of view regarding them; we compare them and we attempt to disengage from them permanent, objective relations. But this necessitates detachment. So long as the reader using the usual optic process of reading identifies himself with the hero of the novel, the character of "Marcel" escapes him; better yet it does not exist on this level. It appears only if I break the complicity which unites me to the writer, only if I consider the book no longer as a confidant but as a confidence, still better as a *document*. This character exists therefore only on the plane of the for-others, and that is the reason why the teachings and the descriptions of "psychological realists" (that is, those French authors who have undertaken an objective, social psychology) are never rediscovered in the lived experience of the subject.

But if character is essentially *for others*, it can not be distinguished from the body as we have described it. To suppose, for example, that temperament is the *cause* of character, that the "sanguine temperament" is the *cause* of irascibility is to posit character as a psychic entity presenting all the aspects of objectivity and yet subjective and *suffered* by the subject. Actually the Other's irascibility is known from the outside and is from the start transcended by my transcendence. In this sense it is not to be distinguished from the "sanguine temperament." In both instances we apprehend the apoplectic redness, the same corporeal aspects, but we transcend these givens differently according to our projects. We shall be dealing with *temperament* if we consider this redness as the manifestation of the *body-as-ground;* that is, by cutting all that binds it to the situation. If we try to understand it *in terms of the corpse,* we shall be able to conduct a physiological and medical study of it. If on the contrary, we consider it by approaching it in terms of the global situation, it will be anger itself or again a promise of anger, or rather an anger in promise—that is, a permanent relation with instrumental-things, a potentiality. Between temperament and character there is therefore only a difference of principle, and character is identical with the body. This is what justifies the attempts of numerous authors to instate a physiognomy as the basis of the studies of character and in particular the fine research of Kretschmer on character and the structure of the body. The character of the Other, in fact, is immediately given to intuition as a synthetic ensemble. This does not mean that we can immediately *describe* it. It would take time to make the differentiated structures appear, to make explicit certain givens which we have immediately apprehended affectively, to transform the global indistinction which is the Other's body into organized form. We can be deceived. It is permissible also to resort to general and discursive knowledge (laws empirically or statistically established in connection with other subjects) in order to *interpret* what we see. But in any case the problem will be only to make explicit and to organize the content of our first intuition in terms of foresight and action. This is without a doubt what is meant by people who insist that "first impressions are not mistaken." In fact from the moment of the first encounter the Other is given entirely and immediately without any veil or mystery. Here to learn is to understand, to develop, and to appreciate.

Nevertheless as the Other is thus given, he is given in what he *is.* Character is not different from facticity—that is, from original contingency. We apprehend the Other as *free,* and we have demonstrated above that *freedom* is an objective quality of the Other as the unconditioned power of modifying situations. This power is not to be distinguished from that which originally constitutes the Other and which is the power to make a situation exist in general. In fact, to be able to modify a situation is precisely to make a situation exist. The Other's objective freedom is only transcendence-transcended; it is, as we have established, freedom-as-object. In this sense the Other appears as the one who must be understood from the standpoint of a situation perpetually modified. This is why his body is always the *past.* In this sense the Other's character is released to us as the surpassed. Even irascibility as the promise of anger is always a surpassed promise. Thus character is given as the Other's facticity as it is accessible to my intuition but also in so far as it *is* only in order to be surpassed. In this sense to "get angry" is already to surpass the irascibility by the very fact that one consents to it; it is to give irascibility a meaning. Anger will appear therefore as the recovery of irascibility by freedom-as-object. This does not mean that we are hereby referred to a subjectivity but only that what we transcend here is not only the Other's facticity but his transcendence, not his being (*i.e.*, his past) but his present and his future. Although the Other's anger appears to me always as a free-anger (which is evident by the very fact that I *pass judgment* on it) I can always transcend it—*i.e.*, stir it up or calm it down; better yet it is by transcending it and only by transcending it that I apprehend it. Thus since the body is the facticity of the transcendence-transcended it is always the body-which-points-beyond-itself; it is at once in space (it is the situation) and in time (it is freedom-as-object). The body for-others is the magic object *par excellence.* Thus the Other's body is always "a body-more-than-body" because the Other is given to me totally and without intermediary in the perpetual surpassing of its facticity. But this surpassing does not refer me to a subjectivity; it is the objective fact that the body—whether it be as organism, as character, or as tool—never appears to me without *surroundings,* and that the body must be determined in terms of these surroundings. The Other's body must not be confused with his objectivity. The Other's objectivity is his transcendence as transcended. The body is the facticity of this transcendence. But the Other's corporeality and objectivity are strictly inseparable.

III. THE THIRD ONTOLOGICAL DIMENSION OF THE BODY

I exist my body: this is its first dimension of being. My body is utilized and known by the Other: this is its second dimension. But in so far as *I am for others,* the Other is revealed to me as the subject for whom I am an object. Even there the question, as we have seen, is of my fundamental relation with the Other. I exist therefore for myself as known by the Other—in particular in my very facticity. I exist for myself as a body known by the Other. This is the third ontological dimension of my body. This is what we are going to study next; with it we shall have exhausted the question of the body's modes of being.

With the appearance of the Other's look I experience the revelation of my being-as-object; that is, of my transcendence as transcended. A me-as-object is revealed to me as an unknowable being, as the flight into an Other which I am with full responsibility. But while I can not know nor even conceive of this "Me" in its reality, at least I am not without apprehending certain of its formal structures. In particular I feel myself touched by the Other in my factual existence; it is my being-there-for-others for which I am responsible.

This *being-there* is precisely the body. Thus the encounter with the Other does not only touch me in my transcendence: in and through the transcendence which the Other surpasses, the facticity which my transcendence nihilates and transcends exists for the Other; and to the extent that I am conscious of existing for the Other I apprehend my own facticity, not only in its non-thetic nihilation, not only in *the existent,* but in its flight towards a being-in-the-midst-of-the-world. The shock of the encounter with the Other is for me a revelation in emptiness of the existence of my body outside as an in-itself for the Other. Thus my body is not given merely as that which is purely and simply lived; rather this "lived experience" becomes—in and through the contingent, absolute fact of the Other's existence— extended outside in a dimension of flight which escapes me. My body's depth of being is for me this perpetual "out-side" of my most intimate "inside."

To the extent that the Other's omnipresence is the fundamental fact, the objectivity of my being-there is a constant dimension of my facticity; I exist my contingency in so far as I surpass it toward my possibles and in so far as it surreptitiously flees me toward an irremediable. My body is there not only as the point of view which I am but again as a point of view on which are actually brought to bear points of view which I could never take; my body escapes me on all sides. This means first that this ensemble of *senses,* which themselves can not be apprehended, is given as apprehended elsewhere and by others. This apprehension which is thus emptily manifested does not have the character of an ontological necessity; its existence can not be derived even from my facticity, but it is an evident and absolute fact. It has the character of a factual necessity. Since my facticity is pure contingency and is revealed to me non-thetically as a factual necessity, the being-for-others of this facticity comes to increase the contingency of this facticity, which is lost and flees from me in an infinity of contingency which escapes me. Thus at the very moment when I *live* my senses as this inner point of view on which I can take no point of view, their being-for-others haunts me: they *are*. For the Other, my senses are as this table or as this tree is for me. They are in the midst of *a world;* they are in and through the absolute flow of *my* world toward the Other. Thus the relativity of my senses, which I can not think abstractly without destroying my world, is at the same time perpetually made present to me through the Other's existence; but it is a pure and inapprehensible appresentation.

In the same way my body is for me the instrument which I am and which can not be utilized by any instrument. But to the extent that the Other in the original encounter transcends my being-there toward his possibilities, this instrument which I am is made-present to me as an instrument submerged in an infinite instrumental series, although I can in no way view this series by "surveying" it. My body as alienated escapes me toward a being-a-tool-among-tools, toward a being-a-sense-organ-apprehended-by-sense-organs, and this is accompanied by an alienating destruction and a concrete collapse of *my* world which flows toward the Other and which the Other will reapprehend in *his* world. When, for example, a doctor listens to my breathing, I *perceive his ear*. To the extent that the objects of the world indicate me as an absolute center of reference, this perceived ear indicates certain structures as forms which I exist on my body-as-a-ground. These structures—in the same upsurge with my being—belong with the purely lived; they are that which I exist and which I nihilate. Thus we have here in the first place the original connection between designation and the lived. The things perceived designate that which I subjectively exist. But I apprehend—on the collapse of the sense object "ear"—the doctor as listening to the sounds in my body, feeling my body with his body, and immediately the lived-designated becomes designated as a *thing outside my subjectivity*, in the midst of a world which is not mine. My body is designated as alienated.

The experience of my alienation is made in and through affective structures such as, for example, *shyness*.[6] To "feel oneself blushing," to "feel oneself sweating," *etc.*, are inaccurate expressions which the shy person uses to describe his state; what he really means is that he is vividly and constantly conscious of his body not as it is for him but as it is *for the Other*. This constant uneasiness, which is the apprehension of my body's alienation as irremediable, can determine psychoses such as ereutophobia (a pathological fear of blushing); these are nothing but the horrified metaphysical apprehension of the existence of my body for the Others. We often say that the shy man is "embarrassed by his own body." Actually this expression is incorrect; I can not be embarrassed by my own body as I exist it. It is my body as it is for the Other which may embarrass me. Yet there too the expression is not a happy one, for I can be embarrassed only by a concrete thing which is presented inside my universe and which hinders me as I try to use other tools. Here the embarrassment is more subtle, for what constrains me is absent. I never encounter my body-for-the-Other as an obstacle; on the contrary, it is because the body is never there, because it remains inapprehensible that it can be *constraining*. I seek to reach it, to master it, by making use of it as an instrument—since it is also given as an *instrument in a world*—in order to give it the form and the attitude which are appropriate. But it is on principle out of reach, and all the acts which I perform in order to appropriate it to myself

[6] In French, *timidité*, which carries also the idea of timidity. Tr.

escape me in turn and are fixed at a distance from me as my body-for-the-Other. Thus I forever act "blindly," shoot at a venture without ever knowing the results of my shooting. This is why the effort of the shy man after he has recognized the uselessness of these attempts will be to suppress his body-for-the-Other. When he longs "not to have a body anymore," to be "invisible," *etc.*, it is not his body-for-himself which he wants to annihilate, but this inapprehensible dimension of the body-alienated.

The explanation here is that we in fact attribute to the body-for-the-Other as much reality as to the body-for-us. Better yet, the body-for-the-Other *is* the body-for-us, but inapprehensible and alienated. It appears to us then that the Other accomplishes for us a function of which we are incapable and which nevertheless is incumbent on us: *to see ourselves as we are.* Language by revealing to us abstractly the principle structures of our body-for-others (even though the existed body is ineffable) impels us to place our alleged mission wholly in the hands of the Other. We resign ourselves to seeing ourselves through the Other's eyes; this means that we attempt to learn our being through the revelations of language. Thus there appears a whole system of verbal correspondence by which we cause our body to be designated for us as it is for the Other by utilizing these designations to denote our body as it is for us. It is on this level that there is effected the analogical identification of the Other's body with mine. It is indeed necessary—if I am to be able to think that "my body is for the Other as the Other's body is for me"—that I have met the Other first in his object-making subjectivity and then as object. If I am to judge the Other's body as an object similar to my body then it is necessary that he has been given to me as an object and that my body has for its part revealed itself to me as possessing an object-dimension. Analogy or resemblance can never at the start constitute the Other's body-as-object and the objectivity of my body; on the contrary, these two object-states must exist beforehand in order that an analogical principle may be brought into play. Here therefore it is language which teaches me my body's structures for the Other.

Nevertheless it is necessary to realize that it is not on the unreflective plane that language with its meanings can slip in between my body and my consciousness which exists it. On this plane the alienation of the body toward the Other and its third dimension of being can only be experienced emptily; they are only an extension of the lived facticity. No concept, no cognitive intuition can be attached to it. The object-state of my body for the Other is not an object for me and can not constitute my body as an object; it is experienced as the flight of the body which I exist. In order that any knowledge which the Other has of my body and which he communicates to me by language may give to my body-for-me a structure of a particular type, it is necessary that this knowledge be applied to an object and that my body already be an object for me. It is therefore on the level of the reflective consciousness that the Other's knowledge can be brought into play; it will not qualify facticity as the pure *existed* of the non-thetic consciousness but rather facticity as the quasi-object apprehended by reflection. It is this conceptual stratum which by inserting itself between the quasi-object and the reflective consciousness will succeed in making an object of the psychic quasi-body. Reflection, as we have seen, apprehends facticity and surpasses it toward an unreal whose esse is a pure *percipi* and which we have named *psychic*. This psychic is constituted. The conceptual pieces of knowledge which we acquire in our history and which all come from our commerce with the Other are going to produce a stratum constitutive of the psychic body.

In short, so far as we suffer our body reflectively we constitute it as a quasi-object by means of an accessory reflection—thus observation comes from ourselves. But as soon
as we *know* the body—*i.e.*, as soon as we apprehend it in a
purely cognitive intuition—we constitute it by that very
intuition with the Other's knowledge (*i.e.*, as it would
never be for us by itself). The knowable structures of our
psychic body therefore simply indicate emptily its perpetual alienation. Instead of living this alienation we constitute it emptily by surpassing the lived facticity toward this
quasi-object which is the psychic-body and by once again
surpassing this quasi-object which is *suffered* toward characters of being which on principle can not be given to me
and which are simply signified.

Let us return, for example, to our description of "physical" pain. We have seen how reflection while "suffering"
physical pain constitutes it as Illness. But we had to stop
midway in our description because we lacked the means to
proceed further. Now, however, we can pursue the point.
The Illness which I suffer I can aim at in its In-itself; that is,
precisely in its being-for-others. At this moment I *know* it;
that is, I aim at it in its dimension of being which escapes
me, at the face which it turns toward Others, and my aim is
impregnated with the wisdom which language has brought
to me;—*i.e.*, I utilize instrumental concepts which come to
me from the Other, and which I should in no case have been
able to form by myself or think of directing upon *my* body.
It is by means of the Other's concepts that I *know* my body.
But it follows that even in reflection I assume the Other's
point of view on my body; I try to apprehend it as if I were
the Other in relation to it. It is evident that the categories
which I then apply to the Illness constitute it *emptily;* that is,
in a dimension which escapes me. Why speak then of *intuition?* It is because despite all, the *body which is suffered*

serves as a nucleus, as matter for the alienating means
which surpass it. The body is this *Illness* which escapes me
toward new characteristics which I establish as limits and
empty schemata of organization. It is thus, for example,
that my *Illness,* suffered as psychic, will appear to me reflectively as sickness *in my stomach.* Let us understand, of
course, that pain "in the stomach" is the stomach itself as
painfully lived. As such before the intervention of the alienating, cognitive stratum, the pain is neither a local sign nor
identification. Gastralgia is the stomach present to consciousness as the pure quality of pain. As we have seen, the
Illness as such is distinguished from all other pain and from
any other illness—and by itself without an intellectual op-
eration of identification or of discrimination. At this level,
how ever, "the stomach" is an inexpressible; it can be neither named nor thought. It is only this suffered figure
which is raised on the ground of the body-existed.
Objectivating empirical knowledge, which presently surpasses the Illness suffered toward the *stomach* named, is the
knowing of a certain objective nature possessed by the
stomach. I know that it has the shape of a bagpipe, that is is
a sack, that it produces juices, and enzymes, that it is in-
closed by a muscular tunica with smooth fibres, *etc.* I can
also know—because a physician has told me—that the
stomach has an ulcer, and again I can more or less clearly
picture the ulcer to myself. I can imagine it as a redness, a
slight internal putrescence; I can conceive of it by means of
analogy with abscesses, fever blisters, pus, canker sores, *etc.*
All this on principle stems from bits of knowledge which I
have acquired from Others or from such knowledge as
Others have of me. In any case all this can constitute my
Illness, not as I enjoy possession of it, but as it escapes me.
The stomach and the ulcer become directions of flight, perspectives of alienation from the object which I possess.

At this point a new layer of existence appears: we have surpassed the lived pain toward the suffered illness; now we surpass the illness toward the *Disease*.[7] The Disease as *psychic* is of course very different from the disease known and described by the physician; it is a state. There is no question here of bacteria or of lesions in tissue, but of a synthetic form of destruction. This form *on principle escapes me;* at times it is revealed to the Other by the "twinges" of pain, by the "crises" of my Illness, but the rest of the time it remains out of reach without disappearing. It is then objectively discernible *for Others*. Others have informed me of it, Others can diagnose it; it is present for Others even though I am not conscious of it. Its true nature is therefore a pure and simple *being-for-others*. When I am not suffering, I speak of it, I conduct myself with respect to it as with respect to an object which on principle is out of reach, for which others are the depositories. If I have hepatitis, I avoid drinking wine so as not to arouse pains in my liver. But my precise goal—not to arouse pains in my liver—is in no way distinct from that other goal—to obey the prohibitions of the physician who revealed the pain to me. Thus another is responsible for *my* disease.

Yet this object which comes to me through others preserves characteristics of a degraded spontaneity deriving from the fact that I apprehend it through my Illness. It is not our intention to describe this new object nor to dwell on its characteristics—its magical spontaneity, its destructive finality, its evil potentiality—on its familiarity with me, and

[7] Sartre in this and in the earlier related passage is contrasting three things—pain, illness, disease. "Pain" refers to the specific aches and twinges, "illness" to the familiar recurrent pattern of these, "disease" to a totality which includes along with pain and illness the cause of them both and which can be diagnosed and named by the physician. The French words are *douleur, mal, and maladie.* Tr.

on its concrete relations with my being (for it is before all else, *my* disease). We wish only to point out that in the disease itself the body is a given: by the very fact that it was the support of the Illness, it is at present the substance of the disease, that which is destroyed by the disease, that across which this destructive form is extended. Thus the injured stomach is present through the gastralgia as the very matter out of which this gastralgia is made. The stomach is there; it is present to intuition and I apprehend it with its characteristics through the suffered pain. I grasp it as *that which is gnawed at*, as a "sack in the shape of a bagpipe," *etc.* I do not see it, to be sure, but I know that it is *my* pain. Hence the phenomena which are incorrectly called "endoscopy." In reality the pain itself tells me nothing about my stomach—contrary to what Sollier claims. But in and by means of the pain, my practical knowledge of it constitutes a stomach-for-others, which appears to me as a concrete and definite absence with exactly those objective characteristics which I have been able to know in it. But on principle the object thus defined stands as the pole of alienation of my pain; it is, on principle, that which I am without having to be it and without being able to transcend it toward anything else. Thus in the same way that a being-for-others haunts my facticity (which is non-thetically lived), so a being-an-object-for-others haunts—as a dimension of escape from my psychic body—the facticity constituted as a quasi-object for an accessory reflection. In the same way pure nausea can be surpassed toward a dimension of alienation; it will then present to me my body-for-others in its "shape," its "bearing," its physiognomy;" it will be given then as *disgust* with my face, disgust with my too-white flesh, with my too-grim expression, *etc.* But we must reverse the terms. I am not disgusted by all this. Nausea *is* all this as non-thetically existed. My knowledge extends my nausea toward that which it is for others. For it is the Other who grasps my nausea, precisely as *flesh* and with the nauseous character of all flesh.

We have not with these observations exhausted the description of the appearances of my body. It remains to describe what we shall call an *aberrant* type of appearance. In actuality I can see my hands, touch my back, smell the odor of my sweat. In this case my hand, for example, appears to me as one object among other objects. It is no longer *indicated* by the environment as a center of reference. It is organized with the environment, and like it indicates my body as a center of reference. It forms a part of the world. In the same way my hand is no longer the instrument which I can not handle along with other instruments; on the contrary, it forms a part of the utensils which I discover in the midst of the world; I can *utilize* it by means of my other hand—for example, when I hold an almond or walnut in my left fist and then pound it with my right hand. My hand is then integrated with the infinite system of utensils-utilized. There is nothing in this new type of appearance which should disturb us or make us retract the preceding statements. Nevertheless this type of appearance must be mentioned. It can be easily explained on condition that we put it *in its proper place* in the order of the appearances of the body; that is, on condition that we examine it last and as a "curiosity" of our constitution. This appearance of my hand means simply that in certain well-defined cases we can adopt with regard to our own body the Other's point of view or, if you like, that our own body can appear to us as the body of the Other. Scholars who have made this appearance serve as a basis for a general theory of the body have radically reversed the terms of the problem and have shown themselves up as understanding nothing about the question. We must realize that this possibility of *seeing* our body is a pure factual given, absolutely contingent. It can be deduced neither from the necessity on the part of the for-itself "to have" a body nor from the factual structures of the body-for-others. One could easily conceive of bodies which could not take any view on themselves; it even appears that this is the case for certain insects which, although provided with a differentiated nervous system and with sense organs, can not employ this system and these organs to know each other. We are dealing therefore with a particularity of structure which we must mention without attempting to deduce it. To have hands, to have hands which can touch each other— these are two facts which are on the same plane of contingency and which as such fall in the province of either pure anatomical description or metaphysics. We can not take them for the foundation of a study of corporeality.

We must note in addition that this appearance of the body does not give us the body as it acts and perceives but only as it is acted on and perceived. In short, as we remarked at the beginning of this chapter, it would be possible to conceive of a system of visual organs such that it would allow one eye to see the other. But the seen eye would be seen as a thing, not as a being of reference. Similarly the hand which I grasp with my other hand is not apprehended as a hand which is grasping but as an apprehensible object. Thus the nature of *our body for us* entirely escapes us to the extent that we can take upon it the Other's point of view. Moreover it must be noted that even if the arrangement of sense organs allows us to see the body as it appears to the Other, this appearance of the body as an instrumental-thing is very late in the child; it is in any case later than the consciousness (of) the body proper and of the world as a complex of instrumentality, it is later than the perception of the body of the Other. The child has known for a long time how to grasp, to draw toward himself, to push away, and to hold on to something before he first learns to pick up his hand and to look at it. Frequent observation has shown that the child of two months does not see his hand as *his* hand. He looks at it, and if it is outside his visual field, he turns his head and seeks his hand with his eyes as if it did not depend on him to bring the hand back within his sight. It is by a series of psychological operations and of syntheses of identification and recognition that the child will succeed in establishing tables of reference between the body-existed and the body-seen. Again it is necessary that the child begin the learning process with the Other's body. Thus the perception of my body is placed chronologically after the perception of the body of the Other.

Considered at its proper place and time and in its original contingency, this appearance of the body does not seem to be capable of giving rise to new problems. The body is the instrument which I am. It is my facticity of being "in-the-midst-of-the-world" in so far as I surpass this facticity toward my being-in-the-world. It is, of course, radically impossible for me to take a global point of view on this facticity, for then I should cease to be it. But why is it so astonishing that certain structures of my body, without ceasing to be a center of reference for the objects of the world, are ordered from a radically different point of view as compared with other objects in such a way that along with the objects they point to one of my sense organs as a partial center of reference raising itself as a figure on the body-as-ground? That my eye should see itself is by nature impossible. But why is it astonishing that my hand touches my eyes? If this seems surprising to us, it is because we have apprehended the necessity for the for-itself to arise as a concrete point of view on the world as if it were an ideal obligation strictly reducible to knowable relations between objects and to simple rules for the development of my achieved knowledge. But instead we ought to see here the necessity of a concrete and contingent existence in the midst of the world.